Simple Friendships

14 Quilts from Exchange-Friendly Blocks

Kim Diehl and Jo Morton

Martingale®
Create with Confidence

Simple Friendships: 14 Quilts from Exchange-Friendly Blocks
© 2017 by Kim Diehl and Jo Morton

Martingale®
19021 120th Ave. NE, Ste. 102
Bothell, WA 98011-9511 USA
ShopMartingale.com

Printed in China
22 21 20 19 18 17   8 7 6 5 4 3 2 1

Library of Congress Cataloging-in-Publication Data
is available upon request.

ISBN: 978-1-60468-735-4

MISSION STATEMENT

We empower makers who use fabric and yarn
to make life more enjoyable.

CREDITS

PUBLISHER AND
CHIEF VISIONARY OFFICER
Jennifer Erbe Keltner

CONTENT DIRECTOR
Karen Costello Soltys

DESIGN MANAGER
Adrienne Smitke

MANAGING EDITOR
Tina Cook

COVER AND
INTERIOR DESIGNER
Regina Giard

ACQUISITIONS EDITOR
Karen M. Burns

PHOTOGRAPHERS
Brent Kane
Adam Albright

TECHNICAL EDITOR
Laurie Baker

COPY EDITOR
Melissa Bryan

ILLUSTRATOR
Missy Shepler

SPECIAL THANKS

*To Cliff and Rosemary Bailey of Snohomish, Washington,
for generously allowing the photography for
this book to take place in their home.*

*To the Garden Barn of Indianola, Iowa, for generously
allowing us to take photographs on location. For more
information, visit TheGardenBarn.com.*

Contents

Introduction . . . 5

The Projects

Star Block
    Twilight . . . 6
    Liberty Star . . . 12

King's Crown Block
    Mocha Berry Crumble . . . 24
    Blueberry Buckle . . . 30

Nine Patch Block
    Apple Cider . . . 36
    Oak Patch . . . 42

Yankee Puzzle Block
    Cobblestone Way . . . 50
    Parkersburg . . . 56

Basket Block
    Berry Baskets . . . 64
    Cake in the Cabin . . . 70

Old Italian Block
    Warm Regards . . . 78
    James River Crossing . . . 92

Sampler Quilts
    Chocolate Factory . . . 98
    Ruby Jubilee . . . 104

Guidelines for Block Exchanges . . . 113
Kim and Jo's Quiltmaking Basics . . . 114
About the Authors . . . 128

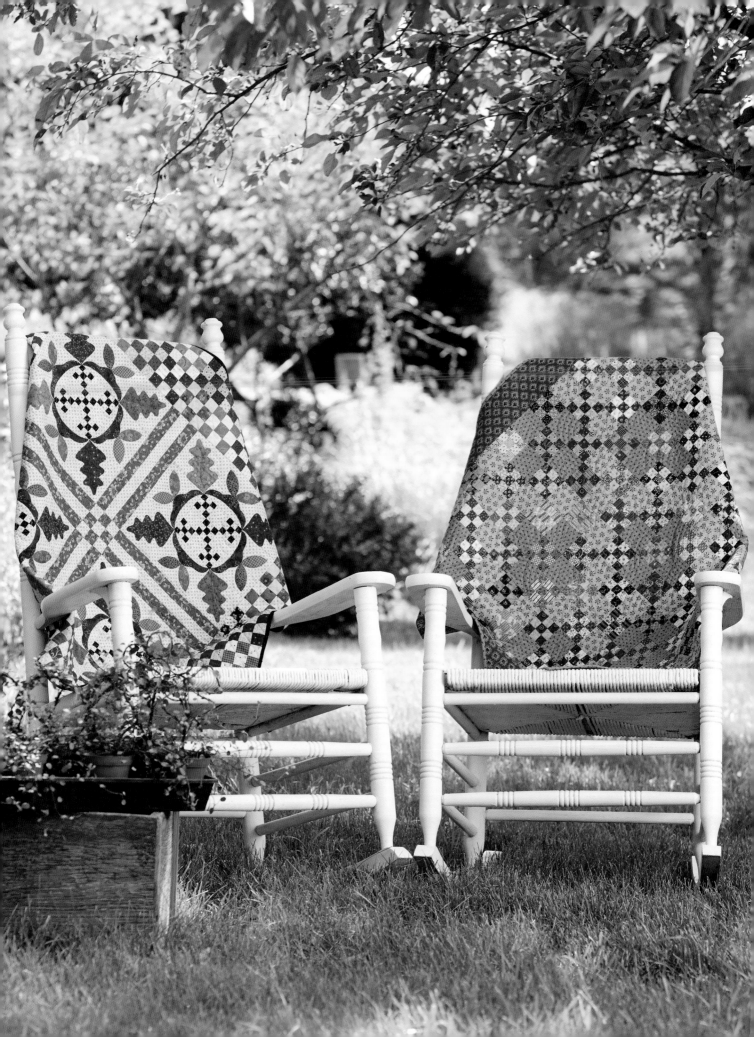

Introduction

Is there anything more fun than making quilts? Absolutely, yes . . . making quilts with friends! And what better way to connect with others who understand our love of creativity and our need to cut up perfectly good fabric?

One of the most wonderful aspects of the art of quiltmaking is that it enables each of us to draw upon our own unique abilities and envision entirely different possibilities. Give 10 different quilters the same block as a starting point, take a step back and let them work some magic, and you'll see 10 very different quilts. So why not embrace the creative nuances that our different perspectives can bring, and swap blocks?

For the projects in this book, we (Kim and Jo) decided to choose six favorite blocks together, and then work independently to see where the creative winds would blow us. We sat down together in Houston over coffee to discuss our guidelines and decided that the sky would be the limit as far as our colors, block sizes, and quilt layouts were concerned. Because, hey, why impose limits? And in the spirit of our "no limits" decision, we gave each other the freedom to tweak our chosen blocks to show just how easy it can be to change one small element and achieve an entirely different design. We love that the guidelines we established during our little "piece talk" resulted in a collection of projects with a fantastic degree of variety—scads of block-swap themes, project sizes, color schemes, techniques . . . and more!

With a few simple parameters, forming a block-swap group can be a snap. You'll find a wealth of information in "Guidelines for Block Exchanges" on page 113, but we'd like to offer a few suggestions right off the bat to help make your exchanges successful. First, always do your best work. Seam allowances aren't subjective, so this means accuracy in piecing your blocks is *super* important. If your finished blocks are too large or too small, no matter how beautiful they are, there's a good chance they'll end up on the scrap heap. And no one wants that!

Second, be sure to follow the established color guidelines for your exchange. For the projects in this book you can choose to use our featured color schemes or create your own, but remember that when you're participating in a swap, it isn't the time to be a trailblazer or stray outside the color box.

And last, be reliable and meet your turn-in date—when the blocks start arriving, it's kind of like the excitement of your birthday and Christmas and the first day of kindergarten all rolled into one, so it's important to be punctual and keep the swap love going.

We hope that the blocks and projects in this book will inspire you to grab your favorite fabrics (and your favorite quilting friends) and have the best time sewing, swapping, and building new lifelong friendships as you stitch your beautiful quilts.

~ *Kim and Jo*

Twilight

The Evening Star blocks in this quilt all have a consistent color palette, but are otherwise scrappy. I used a different blue-and-cream combo for each, making this perfect for a block-exchange quilt. Determine the color palette you want to use, and then each participant will need to select one dark and one light hue for however many blocks she makes. I chose assorted indigo and country blues, combining them with cream shirting prints, but you can change up the color scheme to feature your favorite color or make it completely scrappy and random. ~ Jo

Swap Talk

For my block exchange, I had five participants. We each made five sets of five blocks, for a total of 25 blocks. Each participant kept one of her own block sets and received one set of blocks from each of the other participants. The cutting information provided here is for cutting one block at a time, making it easy for a group to follow. The materials listed include everything you need for constructing all the blocks, in case you're making the quilt on your own.

Materials

Yardage is based on 42" of usable fabric width after prewashing and removing selvages.

Approximately 1 yard *total* of assorted cream shirting prints for Evening Star blocks, sashing cornerstones, and setting triangles

Approximately 1 yard *total* of assorted indigo and medium blue prints for Evening Star blocks, sashing cornerstones, and setting triangles

½ yard of pink print for sashing strips

1⅛ yards of medium blue print for inner border and single-fold binding

1⅛ yards of blue plaid for outer border

1¼ yards of fabric for backing

42" × 42" square of batting

Cutting

You'll need 25 Evening Star blocks to complete the featured quilt. For ease in piecing the blocks, keep the pieces for each block grouped together as you cut them. Keep the pieces for the side setting triangles, the corner setting triangles, and the sashing and borders grouped together for ease in piecing the individual units.

CUTTING FOR 1 EVENING STAR BLOCK

From 1 cream print, cut:
4 squares, 1⅞" × 1⅞"

From 1 indigo print, cut:
1 square, 3¼" × 3¼"

From a 2nd indigo print, cut:
4 squares, 1½" × 1½"

From a 3rd indigo print, cut:
1 square, 2½" × 2½"

Continued on page 8

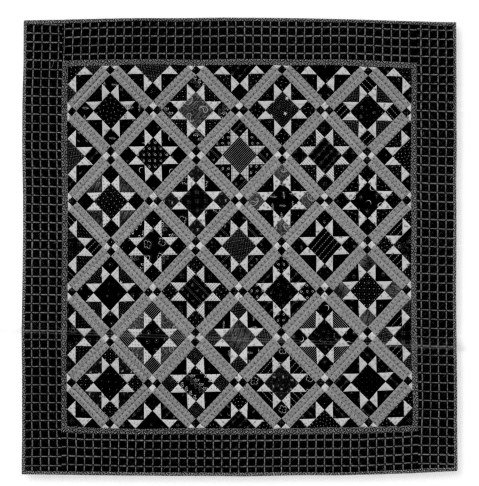

Finished quilt size:
35⅞" × 35⅞"

Finished exchange block size:
4" × 4"

Designed by Jo Morton.
Pieced by Sheri Dowding,
Mary Fornoff, Cindy Hansen,
and Phyllis Masters. Machine
quilted by Maggi Honeyman.

Continued from page 6

ADDITIONAL CUTTING

Cut all pieces across the width of the fabric in the order
given unless otherwise noted.

Side Setting Triangles
From *each of 6* assorted cream prints, cut:
4 squares, 1⅞" × 1⅞" (combined total of 24)

From *each of 6* assorted indigo prints, cut:
1 square, 3¼" × 3¼" (combined total of 6)
1 square, 2⅞" × 2⅞" (combined total of 6); cut
    each square in half diagonally *once* to yield 2
    large triangles (combined total of 12)
2 squares, 1⅞" × 1⅞" (combined total of 12); cut
    each square in half diagonally *once* to yield 4
    small triangles (combined total of 24)
2 squares, 1½" × 1½" (combined total of 12)

Corner Setting Triangles
From 1 cream print, cut:
4 squares, 1⅞" × 1⅞"

From 1 indigo print, cut:
1 square, 3¼" × 3¼"

From *each of 2* different indigo prints, cut:
1 square, 2¾" × 2¾" (combined total of 2); cut
    each square in half diagonally *twice* to yield 4
    small triangles (combined total of 8)

From *each of 2* different indigo prints, cut:
1 square, 2¼" × 2¼" (combined total of 2); cut
    each square in half diagonally *once* to yield 2
    large triangles (combined total of 4)

Sashing, Borders, and Binding
From *each* of 1 indigo and 1 cream print, cut:
5 strips, 1" × 18" (combined total of 10)

From the *lengthwise grain* of the pink print, cut:*
22 strips, 1½" × 15"; crosscut into 64 strips,
    1½" × 4½"

From the *lengthwise grain* of the medium blue print, cut:*
2 strips, 1" × 28⅞"
2 strips, 1" × 29⅞"

From the *lengthwise grain* of the blue plaid, cut:*
2 strips, 3½" × 29⅞"
2 strips, 3½" × 35⅞"

From the medium blue print, cut:
4 single-fold binding strips, 1⅛" × 42" (see
    "Completing the Quilt" on page 11)

*Jo recommends cutting these pieces on the lengthwise grain (parallel to the selvage), because it has the least amount of stretch and will give you nice, straight edges.

Piecing for One Evening Star Block

The instructions that follow will make one block. Use the pieces cut for one block and repeat as many times as needed to make the required number of blocks. Sew all pieces with right sides together using a scant ¼" seam allowance unless otherwise noted. Press the seam allowances as indicated by the arrows or as otherwise specified.

1. Using the cream 1⅞" squares and the indigo 3¼" square, refer to "Jo's No-Waste Flying-Geese Method" (page 115) to make four flying-geese units for the star points. Each unit should measure 1½" × 2½", including the seam allowances.

2. Lay out the flying-geese units from step 1, the four indigo 1½" squares, and the indigo 2½" square in three horizontal rows. Join the units in each row; press.

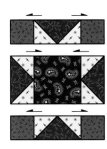

3. Pin and then sew the rows together, matching the seam intersections. Refer to "Jo's Clipping Trick" (page 114) to clip the seam intersections. Press the clipped intersections open and the seam allowances toward the corner and center squares. The pieced block should measure 4½" square, including the seam allowances.

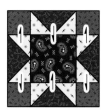

Evening Star block,
4½" x 4½".

Piecing the Side Setting Triangles

1. Repeating the flying-geese technique used for the Evening Star blocks, use the cream 1⅞" squares and indigo 3¼" squares cut for the side setting triangles to make a total of 24 flying-geese units. Each unit should measure 1½" × 2½", including the seam allowances.

2. Using two matching flying-geese units and two matching small triangles from a different indigo than the flying-geese units, join a small triangle to the right edge of one flying-geese unit and to the left edge of the remaining flying-geese unit; press.

3. Join a unit from step 2 to one short edge of a different indigo large triangle. Add a 1½" square that matches the small triangles to the end of the remaining step 2 unit. Sew the unit to the adjacent short edge of the large triangle. Clip the seam intersection. Press the seam intersection open and the seam allowances toward the large triangle. Repeat to make a total of 12 side setting triangles.

Side setting triangle.
Make 12.

Piecing the Corner Setting Triangles

1. Repeating the flying-geese technique, use the indigo 3¼" square and cream 1⅞" squares cut for the corner setting triangles to make a total of four flying-geese units.

2. Using a different indigo than the flying-geese unit, sew an indigo small triangle to each end of a flying-geese unit; press. Add a different indigo large triangle to the top of the unit; press. Repeat to make a total of four corner setting triangles.

Corner triangle.
Make 4.

Piecing the Sashing Cornerstones

1. Sew together the indigo and cream 1" × 18" strips in pairs to make a total of five strip sets; press. Crosscut the strip sets into 80 segments, 1" wide.

Make 5 strip sets.
Cut 80 segments.

2. Join two segments as shown to make a four-patch unit; press. Repeat to make a total of 40 sashing cornerstones measuring 1½" square, including the seam allowances.

Make 40 units,
1½" × 1½".

Assembling the Quilt Top

1. Referring to the quilt assembly diagram on page 11, arrange the blocks, the pink 1½" × 4½" sashing strips, the sashing cornerstones, and the side setting triangles into diagonal rows, paying careful attention to the orientation of the four-patch units. Sew the pieces in each row together; press. Pin and then sew the rows together, matching the seam intersections. The outer sashing cornerstones will extend beyond the edges of the setting triangles. Clip the seam

intersections. Press the clipped intersections open and the seam allowances toward the sashing strips.

Quilt assembly

Rotate the Cornerstones

Notice that in the horizontal rows with four blocks, the sashing cornerstones are oriented with the dark squares running horizontally across the row. In the horizontal rows with three blocks and a side setting triangle on each side, the dark squares run vertically. I think this adds a bit of extra interest to the quilt. ~ Jo

2. Press the quilt top carefully; do not stretch. Trim the sashing cornerstones along the outer edges ¼" from the points of the sashing strips to square up the quilt center. The pieced quilt center should measure 28⅞" square, including the seam allowances.

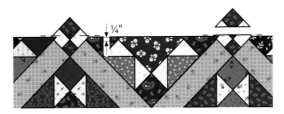

Trim, leaving a ¼" seam allowance.

3. Referring to the diagram below, sew the medium blue 1" × 28⅞" inner-border strips to the right and left sides of the quilt top; press toward the sashing. Join the medium blue 1" × 29⅞" inner-border strips to the remaining sides of the quilt top; press. The quilt top should measure 29⅞" square, including the seam allowances.

4. Sew the blue plaid 3½" × 29⅞" outer-border strips to the right and left sides of the quilt top; press toward the border. Add the blue plaid 3½" × 35⅞" outer-border strips to the remaining sides of the quilt top. The quilt top should measure 35⅞" × 35⅞".

Adding borders

Completing the Quilt

Layer and baste the quilt top, batting, and backing. Quilt the layers. The featured quilt was quilted by machine. Referring to "Jo's Single-Fold Binding" (page 126), or substituting your favorite method, join the medium blue strips into one length and use it to bind the quilt.

Bold colors, strong geometric lines, and classic appliqué motifs combine beautifully in this quilt to pay tribute to our proud heritage of freedom. Best of all, the sprinkling of wool accents provides a perfect opportunity to take up needle and thread and indulge in a bit of hand stitching. ~ Kim

Swap Talk

For this swap, I chose to take the basic Star block one step further and added a square-in-a-square center to make the Mosaic Star block. This change created a fantastic opportunity for incorporating scads of wool pennies in the design, adding an extra element of color and sparkle. Vibrant shades of red and tan work perfectly for the Mosaic Star blocks in this exchange, because the bold colors anchor the design beautifully when paired with the strong appliqué motifs in the quilt.

Materials

Yardage is based on 42" of usable fabric width after prewashing and removing selvages. Fat quarters are 18" × 21", fat eighths are 9" × 21", and chubby sixteenths are 9" × 10½".

28 rectangles, 5" × 10" *each, OR* approximately 1 yard *total* of assorted red prints for Mosaic Star blocks

28 rectangles, 5" × 10" *each, OR* approximately 1¾ yards *total* of assorted tan prints for Mosaic Star blocks

1⅝ yards of black print A for setting blocks, border corners, and binding

2 yards of coordinating tan print for appliqué block backgrounds and setting blocks

⅜ yard of gold print for setting blocks, eagle epaulette appliqués, and border corners

1 chubby sixteenth of light brown print for shield appliqués

1 fat quarter of dark blue print for shield appliqués

1 fat quarter of red print A for eagle head and leg appliqués

1½ yards of red print B for eagle wing and tail appliqués and border

1 fat eighth of black print B for eagle tail appliqués

1 fat eighth of medium blue print for eagle wing and tail appliqués

1 fat quarter of green stripe or print for stem appliqués

44 squares, 1½" × 1½" *each,* of assorted colors of felted wools for large penny appliqués

44 squares, 1" × 1" *each,* of assorted colors of felted wools for small penny appliqués

28 rectangles, 2" × 3½" *each,* of assorted green felted wools for large leaf and blossom-base appliqués

16 rectangles, 1¼" × 3" *each,* of assorted green felted wools for small leaf appliqués

Continued on page 14

Finished quilt size:
58½" × 58½"

Finished exchange block size: 4" × 4"

Designed by Kim Diehl. Pieced by Jan Ragaller and Kim Diehl. Machine and hand appliquéd by Kim Diehl. Machine quilted by Leisa Wiggley.

Continued from page 12

16 squares, 1½" × 1½" *each,* of assorted gold felted wools for shield star appliqués

3¾ yards of fabric for backing

65" × 65" square of batting

Bias bar to make ⅜" stems

Liquid glue for fabric, water-soluble and acid-free (Kim likes the results achieved with Quilter's Choice Basting Glue by Beacon Adhesives)

#12 or #8 perle cotton for stitching the wool appliqués (Kim used Valdani's #12 variegated perle cotton in color H212 Faded Brown)

Size 5 embroidery needle

Supplies for your favorite traditional and wool appliqué methods

Cutting

You'll need 28 Mosaic Star blocks to complete the featured quilt. For ease in piecing the blocks, keep the pieces for each block grouped together as you cut them.

CUTTING FOR 1 MOSAIC STAR BLOCK

From 1 red print 4" × 9" rectangle, cut:
12 squares, 1½" × 1½"

From 1 tan print 5" × 10" rectangle, cut:
1 square, 2½" × 2½"
4 rectangles, 1½" × 2½"
4 squares, 1½" × 1½"

ADDITIONAL CUTTING

Cut all pieces across the width of the fabric in the order given unless otherwise noted. Cutting instructions for the appliqué pieces are provided separately.

From black print A, cut:
5 strips, 4½" × 42"; crosscut into 36 squares,
    4½" × 4½"
1 strip, 3" × 42"; crosscut into 8 squares, 3" × 3"
7 binding strips, 2½" × 42" (see "Completing the
    Quilt" on page 20)
2 squares, 4⅞" × 4⅞"; cut each square in half
    diagonally *once* to yield a total of 4 triangles

From the coordinating tan print, cut:
6 strips, 4½" × 42"; crosscut into:
    20 rectangles, 4½" × 8½"
    8 squares, 4½" × 4½"
2 strips, 16½" × 42"; crosscut into 4 squares,
    16½" × 16½"
2 squares, 4⅞" × 4⅞"; cut each square in half
    diagonally *once* to yield a total of 4 triangles

From the gold print, cut:
1 strip, 4½" × 42"; crosscut into 8 squares,
    4½" × 4½"
1 strip, 3" × 42"; crosscut into 8 squares, 3" × 3"
Reserve the remainder of the print for appliqués.

From the light brown print, cut:
4 rectangles, 1½" × 5½"

From the dark blue print, cut:
4 squares, 5½" × 5½"

From the *bias* of the green stripe or print, cut:
8 strips, 1¼" × 14"

From the *lengthwise grain* of red print B, cut:
4 strips, 5½" × 50"
Reserve the remainder of the fabric for appliqués.

Piecing for One Mosaic Star Block

The instructions that follow will make one block. Use the pieces cut for one block and repeat as many times as needed to make the required number of blocks. Sew all pieces with right sides together using a ¼" seam allowance unless otherwise noted. Press the seam allowances as indicated by the arrows or as otherwise specified.

1. Select a set of pieces cut for one block. Use a pencil and an acrylic ruler to draw a diagonal sewing line from corner to corner on the wrong side of each red 1½" square.

2. Layer prepared red squares onto two opposite corners of the tan 2½" square. Stitch the squares together along the drawn lines. Fold the resulting inner red triangles open, aligning the edges with the corners of the tan square; press. Trim away the layers beneath the top triangles, leaving a ¼" seam allowance. Repeat with the remaining two corners of the tan square to make a pieced square-in-a-square unit measuring 2½" square, including the seam allowances.

Make 1 unit,
2½" x 2½".

3. Referring to step 2, layer, stitch, press, and trim a prepared red square onto each end of a tan 1½" × 2½" rectangle. Repeat for a total of four pieced star-point units measuring 1½" × 2½", including the seam allowances.

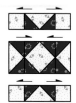

Make 4 units, 1½" x 2½".

4. Lay out the pieced square-in-a-square unit, the four star-point units, and the four tan 1½" squares in three horizontal rows. Join the pieces in each row; press. Join the rows; press. The pieced block should measure 4½" square, including the seam allowances.

Mosaic Star block, 4½" x 4½".

5. Repeat steps 1–4 to make 28 Mosaic Star blocks.

Piecing the Center and Side Units

1. Lay out four pieced Mosaic Star blocks in two horizontal rows of two blocks each. Join the blocks in each row; press. Join the rows; press. Repeat for a total of five quadruple star units measuring 8½" square, including the seam allowances. Reserve the remaining eight Mosaic Star blocks.

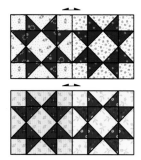 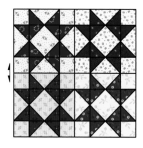

Make 5.

2. Use a pencil and an acrylic ruler to draw a diagonal sewing line from corner to corner on the wrong side of each black print A and gold 4½" square.

3. Repeating the star-point technique used for the Mosaic Star blocks, use the prepared black squares and 16 of the coordinating tan 4½" × 8½" rectangles to make 16 black large star-point units. The units should measure 4½" × 8½", including the seam allowances. Reserve the remaining prepared black print A squares.

Make 16 units, 4½" x 8½".

4. Repeat step 3 using the prepared gold 4½" squares and the remaining four tan 4½" × 8½" rectangles to make four gold large star-point units measuring 4½" × 8½", including the seam allowances.

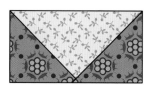

Make 4 units, 4½" x 8½".

5. Join a black triangle and a coordinating tan triangle along the long diagonal edges to make a half-square-triangle unit; press. Trim away the dog-ear points. Repeat to make a total of four half-square-triangle units measuring 4½" square, including the seam allowances.

Make 4 units, 4½" x 4½".

6. To make the center unit, lay out one quadruple star unit, the four gold large star-point units, and the four half-square-triangle units from step 5 in three horizontal rows as shown. Join the pieces in each row; press. Join the rows; press. The center unit should measure 16½" square, including the seam allowances.

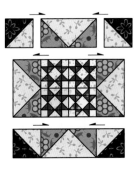 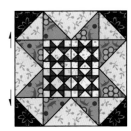

Make 1 center unit,
16½" x 16½".

7. To make the side units, lay out one quadruple star unit, four black large star-point units, two reserved Mosaic Star blocks, and two coordinating tan 4½" squares in three horizontal rows. Join the pieces in each row; press. Join the rows; press. Repeat for a total of four pieced side units measuring 16½" square, including the seam allowances.

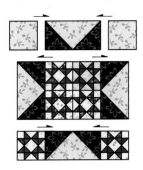 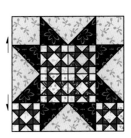

Make 4 side units,
16½" x 16½".

Appliquéing the Mosaic Star Blocks

Patterns for the large and small penny appliqué patterns are provided on page 22. Refer to "Kim's Wool-Appliqué Technique" on page 122 or use your favorite method.

1. Using your favorite wool appliqué method, cut and prepare:
   - 44 large pennies from the assorted wool 1½" squares
   - 44 small pennies from the assorted wool 1" squares

2. Work from the bottom layer to the top to stitch a large and small penny to the center of each Mosaic Star block. Reserve the remaining pennies for the corner units.

Piecing the Corner Units

Layer a reserved marked black print A 4½" square onto one corner of a coordinating tan 16½" square. Stitch, press, and trim as previously instructed to add a black corner triangle. Repeat for a total of four pieced corner units measuring 16½" square, including the seam allowances.

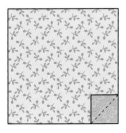 

Make 4.

Appliquéing the Eagles to the Corner Units

The eagle appliqué patterns are provided on pages 21–23. Refer to "Kim's Invisible Machine-Appliqué Technique" on page 116 or use your favorite method.

1. Join a light brown 1½" × 5½" rectangle to one side of a dark blue 5½" square. Press the seam allowances toward the light brown. Repeat to make a total of four units. From these pieced units, cut four shield appliqués, aligning the marked line of the shield pattern with the seams of the pieced units.

2. Cut and prepare the following appliqués. To make complete patterns of the medium and large tail shapes, fold a piece of freezer paper in half (5" × 6" rectangle for medium tail and 7" square for large tail) and finger-press he crease. Unfold and align the crease with the pattern dashed line. Trace the pattern, refold the paper, and cut out the shape on the solid line; unfold. Patterns without grain-line arrows should be positioned on and cut from the fabric to make the best use of the print.

   - 4 heads from red A
   - 4 legs and 4 reversed legs from red A
   - 4 wings and 4 reversed wings from red B
   - 4 large tails from red B
   - 4 medium tails from black B
   - 4 small tails from medium blue
   - 8 wing tops from medium blue
   - 8 epaulettes from gold

3. With right sides together, fold each pieced corner unit in half diagonally, with the fold running through the black triangle corner, and lightly press a center crease.

4. Using the pictured quilt as a guide, lay out one eagle head, one wing and one reversed wing, two blue wing tops, one leg and one reversed leg, one large tail, and one shield. Use the pressed background crease to center the pieces onto the corner unit, tucking the raw eagle edges underneath the shield and adjusting the angle of the wings as needed. When you're pleased with the arrangement and are sure all design elements fit the block space properly, pin or baste all of the red eagle pieces in place; remove the shield and wing tops. Stitch the appliqués to the corner unit, leaving approximately ¾" unstitched on the wings as indicated on the pattern, and leaving the inner talon of each leg unstitched to later be positioned on top of the stems.

5. Reposition the wing tops so that they overlap the wings and form a smooth wing outline; pin or baste. Stitch the wing tops in place, again leaving approximately ¾" unstitched as indicated on the pattern for positioning the epaulettes.

6. Work from the bottom layer to the top to position, baste, and stitch the medium and small tail pieces onto the large tail. Next, reposition the shield, ensuring it covers all raw edges of the eagle; baste and stitch.

7. Position an epaulette onto each wing, ensuring the raw edges of the wings and wing tops are covered. Tuck the raw ends of the epaulettes under the unstitched portions of the wings and wing tops, shaping the pieces to form a smooth silhouette; stitch.

8. Repeat steps 4–7 to appliqué four corner units.

Assembling the Quilt Top

1. Lay out the four black-star side units, the gold-star center unit, and the four appliquéd Eagle blocks in three horizontal rows, referring to the quilt assembly diagram below.

2. Join the pieces in each row. Press the seam allowances of the top and bottom rows toward the corner units. Press the seam allowances of the middle row toward the center unit.

3. Join the rows. Press the seam allowances toward the top and bottom rows. The quilt center should now measure 48½" square, including the seam allowances.

Quilt assembly

Completing the Appliqué

Patterns for the appliqués are provided on pages 21–23.

1. With *wrong* sides together, fold each of the green bias strips in half lengthwise and use a scant ¼" seam allowance to stitch along the long raw edges to make tubes. Use the bias bar to press the tubes flat, centering the seam allowances so they'll be hidden from the front. Apply small dots of liquid fabric glue underneath the pressed seam allowance of each stem at approximately ½" intervals, and use a hot, dry iron to heat set the seams from the back of the stem and anchor them.

2. Measure and cut away a 2½" length from each stem. For each remaining long stem, apply a small amount of liquid glue (or fabric glue stick, if you prefer) to the wrong side at one end. Fold the glued end over approximately ¼" to hide the raw edge on the back of the stem, and heat set with a hot, dry iron.

3. Cut and prepare the following wool appliqués:
   - 16 stars from assorted gold wool squares
   - 12 large leaves and 12 reversed large leaves from assorted green wools
   - 8 small leaves and 8 reversed small leaves from assorted green wools
   - 16 blossom bases from assorted green wools

Adding the Border

1. Lay out two black print A and two gold 3" squares in two horizontal rows of two squares each to form a four-patch unit. Join the squares in each row, and then join the rows. Press the seam allowances to one side. Repeat for a total of four four-patch units measuring 5½" square, including the seam allowances.

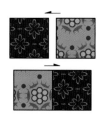

Make 4 units,
5½" x 5½".

4. Working on one corner of the quilt top and using the pictured quilt as a guide, lay out a long stem on each side of the eagle with the finished ends down, and positioning the unstitched eagle talons so they slightly rest on top of the stems; baste in place. Position a 2½" stem near the bottom of each long stem, tucking the raw ends underneath the long stems; baste. Lay out and baste three large leaves along one long stem and three reversed large leaves along the remaining stem, tucking the ends underneath the stems by about ⅛". Position two small leaves along one stem and two small reversed leaves along the remaining stem, with the tips just resting against the stems; baste. Appliqué the stems and eagle talons in place, and then stitch the wool appliqués.

5. Position and stitch a blossom base to each raw stem end, overlapping the stems by approximately ¼". Work from the bottom layer to the top to position and stitch four large and four small pennies, placing them just above the blossom bases.

6. Position, baste, and stitch four stars onto the shield.

7. Repeat steps 4–6 to complete the appliqué on each corner unit of the quilt top.

2. Measure the length of the quilt top through the center and trim the red 5½" × 50" strips to this length. Join two of the strips to the right and left sides of the quilt top. Press the seam allowances toward the border. Sew a four-patch unit to each end of the two remaining red strips. Press the seam allowances toward the strips. Join these strips to the remaining sides of the quilt top. Press the seam allowances toward the border.

Completing the Quilt

Layer and baste the quilt top, batting, and backing. Quilt the layers. The featured quilt was machine quilted with feathered wreaths that merge from the open background areas into the red border strips, and the remaining background areas were filled with a small stipple design. The large gold and black star points were echo quilted with concentric straight lines, and the Mosaic Stars were outlined. Clamshell and feather designs were stitched onto the eagles for texture, and a small crosshatch was quilted onto the blue wing tops. The red border was stitched with a serpentine feather design and the remaining open border areas were filled with repeating straight lines. Referring to "Kim's Chubby Binding" on page 127, or substituting your favorite method, use the black binding strips to bind the quilt.

Liberty Star

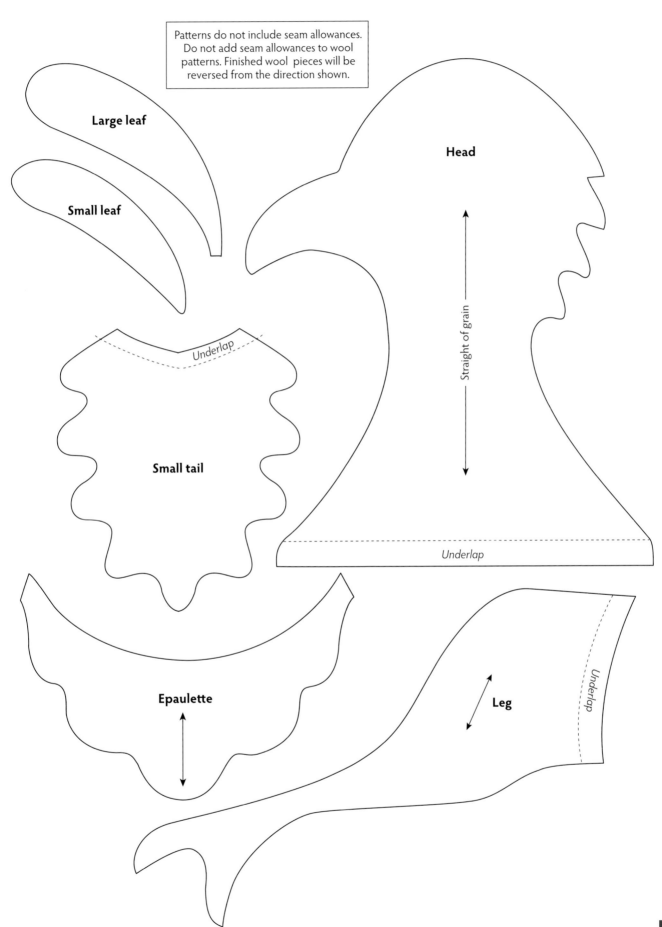

Patterns do not include seam allowances.
Do not add seam allowances to wool
patterns. Finished wool pieces will be
reversed from the direction shown.

Large leaf

Small leaf

Head

Straight of grain

Underlap

Small tail

Underlap

Epaulette

Leg

Underlap

21

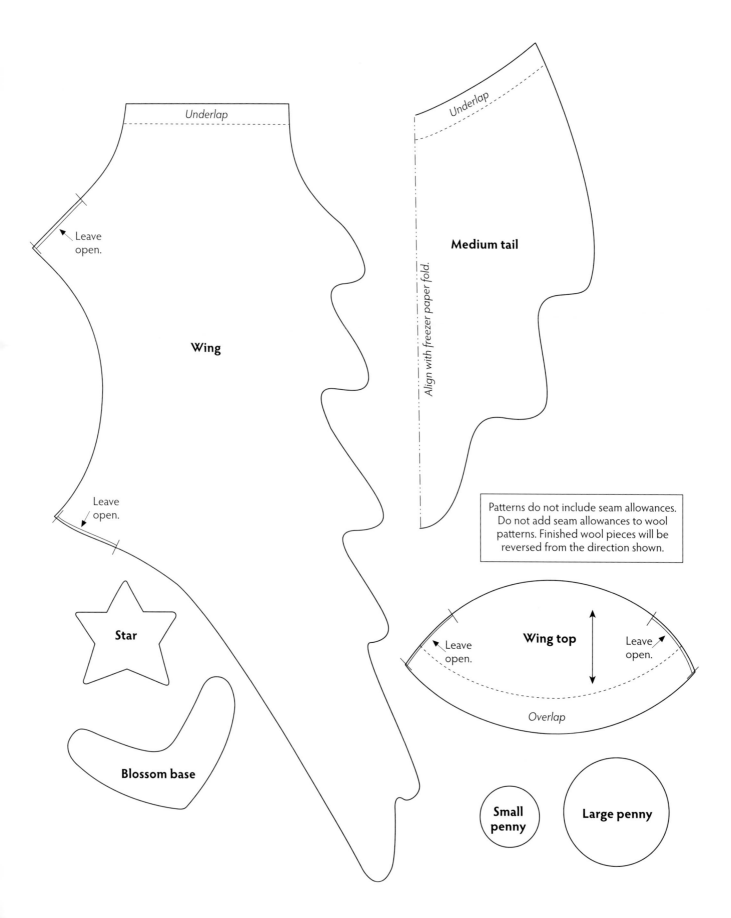

Underlap

Leave
open.

Wing

Leave
open.

Star

Blossom base

Underlap

Medium tail

Align with freezer paper fold.

Patterns do not include seam allowances.
Do not add seam allowances to wool
patterns. Finished wool pieces will be
reversed from the direction shown.

Leave
open.

Wing top

Leave
open.

Overlap

Small
penny

Large penny

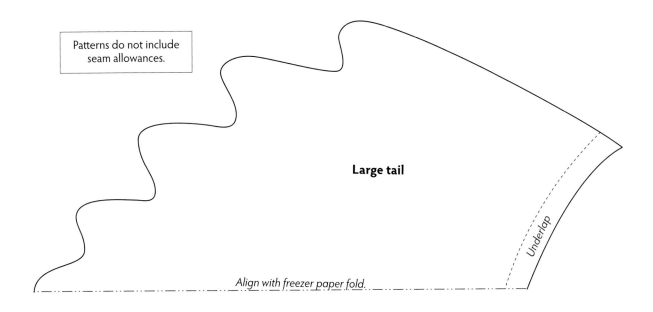

Patterns do not include seam allowances.

Large tail

Underlap

Align with freezer paper fold.

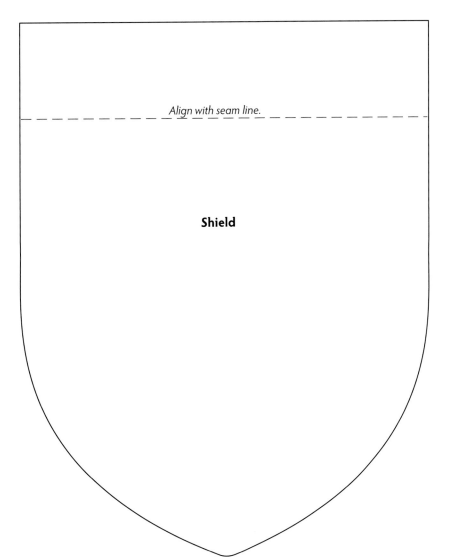

Align with seam line.

Shield

Yummy prints in assorted shades of chocolate, raspberry, and cream create a simple yet striking palette when stitched into this patchwork project. Perfectly sized to grace your favorite tabletop, this little quilt is fun to stitch and even easier to live with.
~ Kim

Swap Talk

For the King's Crown blocks in this exchange, I chose the classic color scheme of pink, brown, and cream. Using prints with a variety of light, medium, and dark values, rather than similar medium hues, adds depth and interest to the finished quilt.

Materials

Yardage is based on 42" of usable fabric width after prewashing and removing selvages. Fat quarters are 18" × 21", fat eighths are 9" × 21", and charm squares are 5" × 5".

13 rectangles, 4" × 10" *each*, of assorted pink prints for King's Crown blocks

13 rectangles, 4" × 6" *each*, of assorted brown prints for King's Crown blocks

13 squares, 5" × 5" *each*, of assorted cream shirting prints for King's Crown blocks

1⅛ yards of brown stripe or print for setting blocks, outer border, and binding

1 fat quarter of cream print for setting blocks

1 fat eighth of pink floral for inner border

1 charm square of pink print for inner border

1 yard of fabric for backing

34" × 34" square of batting

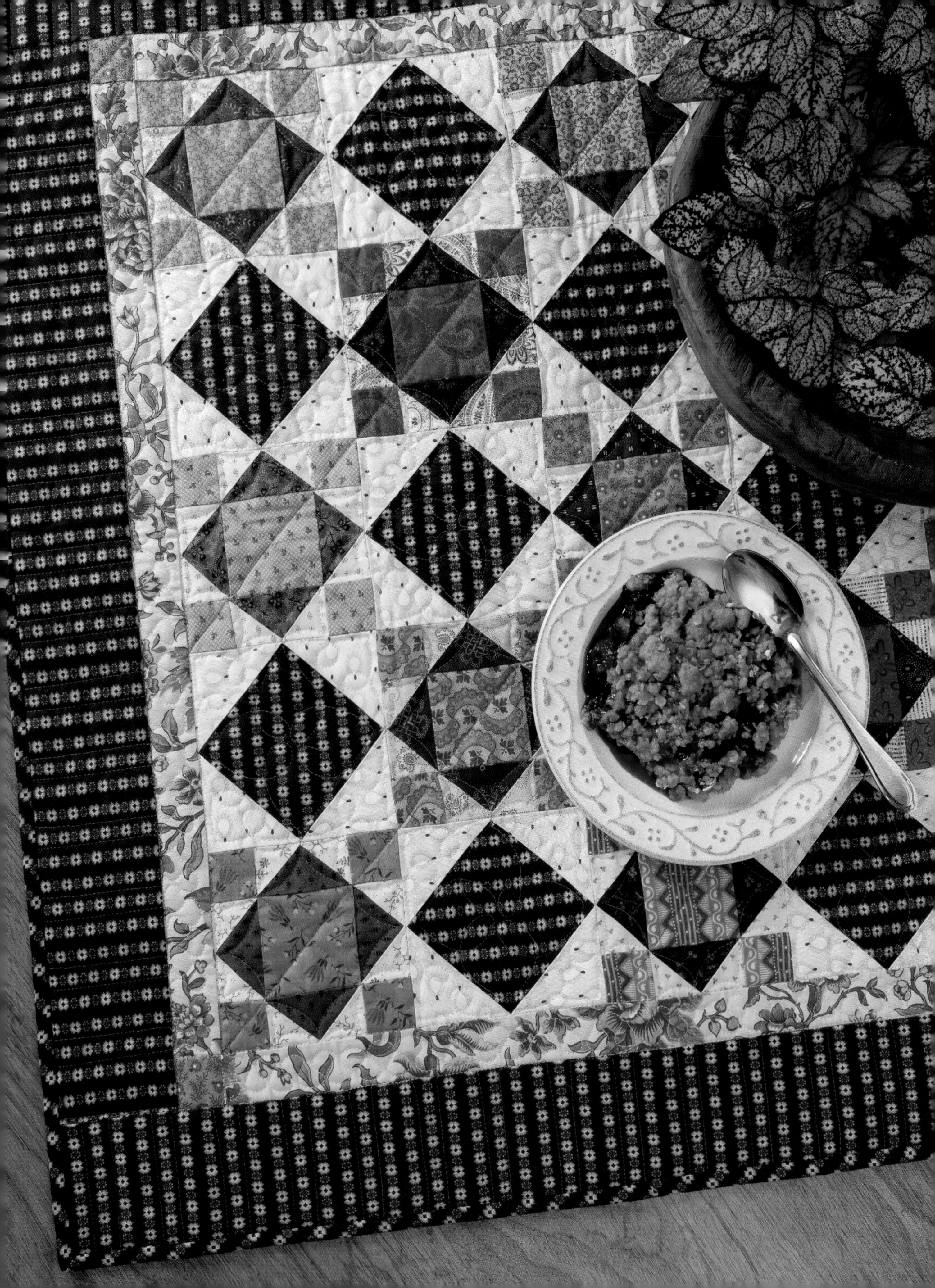

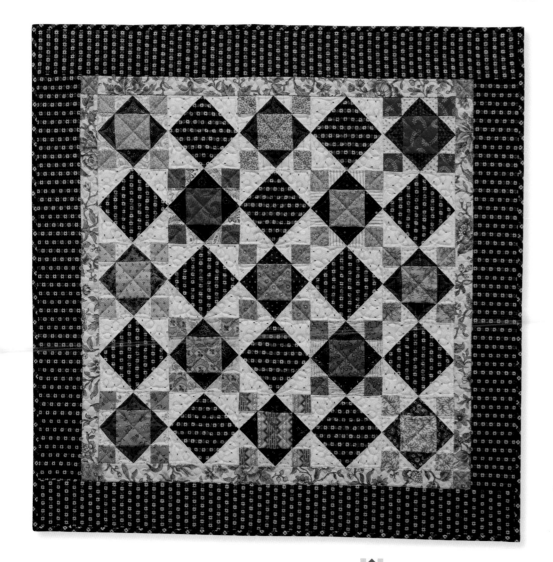

Finished quilt size:
27½" × 27½"

**Finished exchange
block size:** 4" × 4"

*Designed by Kim
Diehl. Pieced by
Jennifer Martinez
and Kim Diehl.
Machine quilted by
Karen Brown.*

Cutting

*You'll need 13 King's Crown blocks to complete the
featured quilt. For ease in piecing the blocks, keep the
pieces for each block grouped together as you cut them.*

CUTTING FOR
1 KING'S CROWN BLOCK

From 1 pink print 4" × 10" rectangle, cut:
1 square, 2½" × 2½"
4 squares, 1½" × 1½"

From 1 brown print 4" × 6" rectangle, cut:
4 rectangles, 1½" × 2½"

From 1 cream shirting print 5" square, cut:
8 squares, 1½" × 1½"

ADDITIONAL CUTTING

*Cut all pieces across the width of the fabric in the order
given unless otherwise noted.*

From the brown stripe or print, cut:
2 strips, 4½" × 42"; crosscut into 12 squares,
    4½" × 4½"
4 strips, 3" × 42"; crosscut into:
    2 strips, 3" × 22½"
    2 strips, 3" × 27½"
Enough 2½"-wide *bias* strips to make a 120"
    length of binding when joined end to end (see
    "Completing the Quilt" on page 29)

From the cream print, cut:
48 squares, 2½" × 2½"

From the pink floral, cut:
4 strips, 1½" × 20½"

From the pink print charm square, cut:
4 squares, 1½" × 1½"

Piecing for One King's Crown Block

The instructions that follow will make one block. Use the pieces cut for one block and repeat as many times as needed to make the required number of blocks. Sew all pieces with right sides together using a ¼" seam allowance unless otherwise noted. Press the seam allowances as indicated by the arrows or as otherwise specified.

1. Select a set of pieces cut for one block. Use a pencil and an acrylic ruler to draw a diagonal sewing line from corner to corner on the wrong side of each cream shirting 1½" square.

2. Layer a prepared cream square onto one end of a brown print 1½" × 2½" rectangle. Stitch the pair together along the drawn line. Fold the resulting inner triangle open, aligning the corner with the corner of the brown rectangle; press. Trim away the excess layers beneath the top triangle, leaving a ¼" seam allowance. Repeat on the remaining end of the brown rectangle to make a mirror-image point. Repeat for a total of four flying-geese units measuring 1½" × 2½", including the seam allowances.

Make 4 units,
1½" x 2½".

3. Lay out the pink 2½" square, the pink 1½" squares, and the step 2 flying-geese units in three horizontal rows. Join the pieces in each row; press. Join the rows; press. The pieced block should measure 4½" square, including the seam allowances.

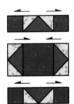

King's Crown block,
4½" x 4½".

4. Repeat steps 1–3 to make 13 King's Crown blocks for the quilt.

Piecing the Setting Blocks

1. Use a pencil and an acrylic ruler to draw a diagonal sewing line from corner to corner on the wrong side of each cream print 2½" square.

2. Referring to step 2 of "Piecing for One King's Crown Block" on page 27, layer, stitch, press, and trim two prepared cream squares onto opposite corners of a brown stripe 4½" square. Repeat with the remaining two corners of the brown square. Repeat to make a total of 12 pieced setting blocks measuring 4½" square, including the seam allowances.

Make 12 blocks,
4½" x 4½".

Assembling the Quilt Top

1. Using the pictured quilt as a guide, lay out three King's Crown blocks and two setting blocks in alternating positions. Join the blocks to make an A row; press. Repeat for a total of three pieced A rows measuring 4½" × 20½", including the seam allowances.

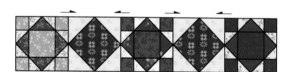

Row A.
Make 3.

2. Repeat step 1 using three setting blocks and two King's Crown blocks, reversing the positions of the blocks to make a B row. Repeat for a total of two B rows measuring 4½" × 20½", including the seam allowances.

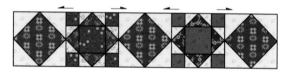

Row B.
Make 2.

3. Referring to the quilt assembly diagram on page 29, lay out the A and B rows in alternating positions. Join the rows. Press the seam allowances open. The pieced quilt center should measure 20½" square, including the seam allowances.

4. Join the floral 1½" × 20½" inner-border strips to the right and left sides of the quilt center. Press the seam allowances toward the border. Join a pink 1½" square to each end of the remaining floral 1½" × 20½" inner-border strips. Press. Join these pieced border strips to the remaining sides of the quilt center; press.

5. Join the brown stripe 3" × 22½" outer-border strips to the right and left sides of the quilt top. Press. Join the brown stripe 3" × 27½" outer-border strips to the remaining sides of the quilt top. Press.

Completing the Quilt

Layer and baste the quilt top, batting, and backing. Quilt the layers. The featured quilt was machine quilted with a large X from corner to corner in the King's Crown blocks; arced lines were quilted along the remaining seams of the King's Crown blocks. The setting blocks were quilted with overlapping loops in the center square, and a variation of the looped design was used in each corner triangle. A ribbon candy design was stitched onto the inner floral border, and an X was stitched onto each corner square. The outer border was stitched with straight lines between the stripes, alternating two stripes and then one stripe, to create a repeating pattern of wide and narrow rectangles. Referring to "Kim's Chubby Binding" on page 127, or substituting your favorite method, use the brown binding strips to bind the quilt.

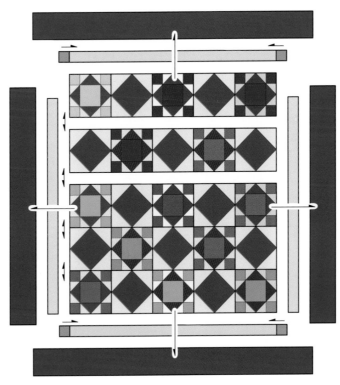

Quilt assembly

Blueberry Buckle

What could be better than fresh-baked blueberry buckle? A sweet little quilt named for this favorite summertime treat! That, and having your quilting friends help out in making the quilt. Sure you can make all 16 blocks needed by yourself, but it sure is fun to see what your friends "cook up" for your quilt! ~ Jo

Swap Talk

Before swapping, plan your color scheme. To replicate the look of the quilt shown, think blended or low contrast. I used teal blue prints ranging from light to dark, creamy shirting prints (no bright whites), and neutral tans to medium and darker brown prints. You'll need four prints per King's Crown block. Choose four blues, or four browns, or a mixture of both. Personally, I like the mix.

Materials

Yardage is based on 42" of usable fabric width after prewashing and removing selvages. Fat quarters are 18" × 21".

Approximately ⅓ yard *total* of assorted cream shirting prints for blocks

Approximately ½ yard *total* of assorted light, medium, and dark teal and brown prints for blocks and cornerstones

1 fat quarter of tan-and-blue plaid for sashing strips

⅝ yard of medium brown print for inner border

⅞ yard of tan floral for outer border

¼ yard of teal print for single-fold binding

1 yard of fabric for backing

33" × 33" square of batting

Finished quilt size:
26½" × 26½"

**Finished exchange block
size:** 4" × 4"

*Designed by Jo Morton.
Pieced by Sheri Dowding,
Mary Fornoff, Cindy
Hansen, and Phyllis Masters.
Machine quilted by
Maggi Honeyman.*

Cutting

*You'll need 16 King's Crown blocks to complete the
featured quilt. For ease in piecing the blocks, keep the
pieces for each block grouped together as you cut them.*

CUTTING FOR
1 KING'S CROWN BLOCK

From 1 cream print, cut:
4 squares, 1⅞" × 1⅞"

From 1 teal or brown print, cut:
1 square, 3¼" × 3¼"

From a second teal or brown print, cut:
4 squares, 1½" × 1½"

From a third teal or brown print, cut:
1 square, 2½" × 2½"

ADDITIONAL CUTTING

*Cut all pieces across the width of the fabric in the order
given unless otherwise noted.*

**From the *lengthwise grain* of the tan-and-blue
plaid, cut:***
24 rectangles, 1½" × 4½"

From the assorted dark teal prints, cut:
9 squares, 1½" × 1½"

**From the *lengthwise grain* of the medium brown
print, cut:***
4 strips, 1½" × 19½"

From 1 dark teal print, cut:
4 squares, 1½" × 1½"

From the *lengthwise grain* of the tan floral, cut:*
2 strips, 3" × 21½"
2 strips, 3" × 26½"

From the teal print for binding, cut:
3 single-fold binding strips, 1⅛" × 42" (see "Completing the Quilt" on page 35)

*Jo recommends cutting these pieces along the lengthwise grain of the fabric (parallel to the selvage), because it has the least amount of stretch and will give you nice, straight edges.

Piecing for One King's Crown Block

The instructions that follow will make one block. Use the pieces cut for one block and repeat as many times as needed to make the required number of blocks. Sew all pieces with right sides together using a scant ¼" seam allowance unless otherwise noted. Press the seam allowances as indicated by the arrows or as otherwise specified.

1. Using the cream 1⅞" squares and the teal or brown 3¼" square, refer to "Jo's No-Waste Flying-Geese Method" (page 115) to make four flying-geese units. The units should be 1½" × 2½", including the seam allowances.

2. Lay out the four flying-geese units from step 1, four matching teal or brown 1½" squares, and the different teal or brown 2½" square in three horizontal rows. Join the units in each row.

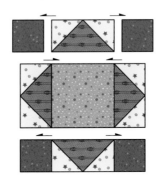

3. Pin and then sew the rows together, matching the seam intersections. Refer to "Jo's Clipping Trick" (page 114) to clip the seam intersections. Press. The block should measure 4½" square, including the seam allowances.

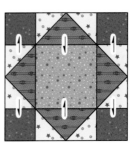

King's Crown block,
4½" × 4½".

4. Repeat steps 1–3 to make 16 King's Crown blocks.

Assembling the Quilt Top

1. Referring to the quilt assembly diagram below, lay out the blocks, the tan plaid 1½" × 4½" sashing strips, and the dark teal 1½" sashing cornerstones in four block rows and three sashing rows. Each block row should have four blocks and three sashing strips; each sashing row should have four sashing strips and three sashing cornerstones. Sew the pieces in each block row and each sashing row together. Press.

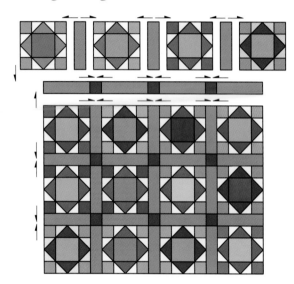

Quilt assembly

Sewing in Quadrants

I often sew my pieces together in quadrants rather than rows. It sounds intimidating but it really isn't. Think of it as making large four-patch units. One thing I really like about joining the pieces this way is that you only have one long seam to sew to join the quadrants. If a quilt is really large, I may assemble the pieces in nine-patch units. Give it a try! It's the only way you'll know if you like it. ~ Jo

2. Join the rows, matching the seam intersections. Clip the seam intersections. Press the seam intersections open and the seam allowances toward the sashing strips. The pieced quilt top should measure 19½" square, including the seam allowances.

3. Refer to the adding borders diagram on page 35 to sew the medium brown 1½" × 19½" inner-border strips to the right and left sides of the quilt top. Press the seam allowances toward the border. Add a dark teal 1½" square to each end of the remaining medium brown 1½" × 19½" inner-border strips. Press the seam allowances toward the strips. Join these pieced border strips to the remaining sides of the quilt top. Clip the seam intersections and press the seam allowances toward the medium brown strips. The quilt top should now measure 21½" square, including the seam allowances.

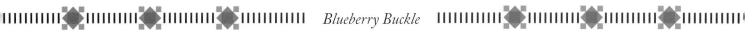
4. Sew the tan floral 3" × 21½" outer-border strips to the right and left sides of the quilt top. Press the seam allowances toward the outer border. Join the tan floral 3" × 26½" outer-border strips to the remaining sides of the quilt top. Press the seam allowances toward the outer border.

Completing the Quilt

Layer and baste the quilt top, batting, and backing. Quilt the layers. The featured quilt was quilted by machine. Referring to "Jo's Single-Fold Binding" (page 126), or substituting your favorite method, join the teal strips into one length and use it to bind the quilt.

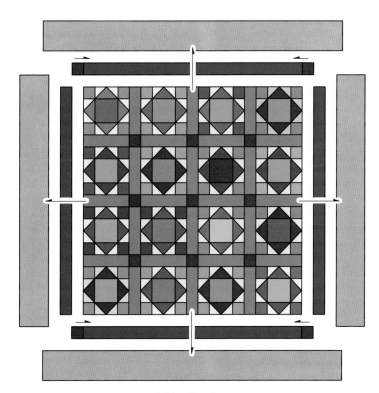

Adding borders

To make this quilt, which is based on an antique, I used Nine Patch blocks from an exchange I did with a group of 10 friends. We exchanged 22 blocks per person, giving us a total of 220 blocks each. I used 113 blocks for this quilt, so I have 107 more to set together in a different way. Because this quilt has so many blocks, it's easiest to make them in batches of matching blocks—whether you're doing them for a friendship trade or making them all for yourself. ~ Jo

Swap Talk

Here are the instructions I shared with my group about color choices:

"All blocks should be two colors: one light and one dark. For the lights, no white shirtings. You can use cream or toast-like prints. For darks, use anything from the Civil War era, but nothing that reads as black. Feel free to use some indigo. You can use chrome yellow or double pinks, but sparingly."

Of course, you can feel free to choose whatever colors you like. But for a group exchange, it's good to provide some guidance to be sure that the blocks you get in the exchange are blocks you'll be able to use.

Materials

Yardage is based on 42" of usable fabric width after prewashing and removing selvages.

Approximately 1⅓ yards *total* of assorted dark prints for Nine Patch blocks

Approximately 1⅓ yards *total* of assorted light prints for Nine Patch blocks

⅜ yard of medium brown print for setting squares

½ yard of taupe print for setting squares

1⅓ yards of red print for border

¼ yard of tan print for single-fold binding*

2⅝ yards of fabric for backing

47" × 47" square of batting

*For double-fold binding, you'll need ½ yard of fabric.

Cutting

You'll need 113 Nine Patch blocks to complete the featured quilt. For ease in piecing the blocks, keep the pieces for each pair of blocks grouped together as you cut them.

CUTTING FOR 2 NINE PATCH BLOCKS

From the *lengthwise grain* of 1 dark print, cut:*
2 rectangles, 1¼" × 5½"
1 rectangle, 1¼" × 3"

From the *lengthwise grain* of 1 light print, cut:*
1 rectangle, 1¼" × 5½"
2 rectangles, 1¼" × 3"

Continued on page 38

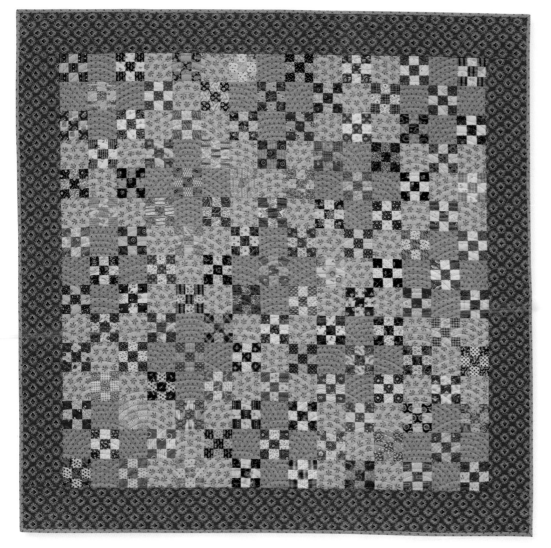

Finished quilt size:
40¾" × 40¾"

**Finished exchange
block size:** 2¼" × 2¼"

*Designed by
Jo Morton. Pieced by
Sheri Dowding,
Mary Fornoff,
Cindy Hansen, and
Phyllis Masters.
Machine quilted by
Maggi Honeyman.*

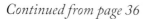

Continued from page 36

ADDITIONAL CUTTING

*Cut all pieces across the width of the fabric in the order
given unless otherwise noted.*

From the medium brown print, cut:
4 strips, 2¾" × 42"; crosscut into 52 squares,
  2¾" × 2¾"

From the taupe print, cut:
5 strips, 2¾" × 42"; crosscut into 60 squares,
  2¾" × 2¾"

From the *lengthwise grain* of the red print, cut:*
2 strips, 3¾" × 34¼"
2 strips, 3¾" × 40¾"

From the tan print, cut:
5 single-fold binding strips, 1⅛" × 42" (see
  "Completing the Quilt" on page 41)

**Jo recommends cutting these pieces on the lengthwise
grain of the fabric (parallel to the selvage), because it
has the least amount of stretch and will give you nice,
straight edges.*

Piecing for Two Nine Patch Blocks

The instructions that follow will make two matching blocks. Use the pieces cut for one pair of blocks and repeat as many times as needed to make the required number of blocks. Sew all pieces with right sides together using a scant ¼" seam allowance unless otherwise noted. Because the blocks are so small, be sure your seam allowance is accurate; if it's too wide, the blocks will be noticeably undersized. Press the seam allowances as indicated by the arrows or as otherwise specified.

1. Using the 1¼" × 5½" rectangles, sew a dark rectangle to each long edge of the light rectangle to make strip set A; press. Crosscut the strip set into four segments, 1¼" wide.

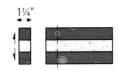

1¼"

Strip set A.
Cut 4 segments, 1¼" x 2¾".

2. Using the 1¼" × 3" rectangles, sew a light rectangle to each long edge of a dark rectangle to make strip set B; press. Crosscut the strip set into two segments, 1¼" wide.

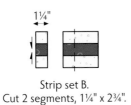

1¼"

Strip set B.
Cut 2 segments, 1¼" x 2¾".

3. Pin and then sew an A segment to each long edge of a B segment, matching the seam intersections; press. Repeat to make a total of two blocks. Each pieced block should measure 2¾" square, including the seam allowances.

Make 2 blocks,
2¾" x 2¾".

4. Repeat steps 1–3 to make 114 Nine Patch blocks (one will be extra).

Piecing the Double Nine Patch Blocks

1. Arrange five Nine Patch blocks and four medium brown 2¾" squares in three horizontal rows. Sew the pieces in each row together; press.

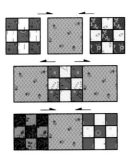

2. Pin and then sew the rows together, matching the seam intersections. Refer to "Jo's Clipping Trick" (page 114) to clip the seam intersections. Press the clipped intersections open and the seam allowances toward the medium brown squares. The block should

measure 7¼" square, including the seam allowances. Repeat to make a total of 13 A blocks.

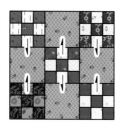

Block A.
Make 13 blocks, 7¼" x 7¼".

3. Arrange four Nine Patch blocks and five taupe 2¾" squares in three horizontal rows. Sew the pieces in each row together; press.

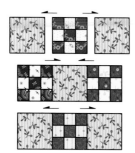

4. Pin and then sew the rows together, matching the seam intersections. Clip the seam intersections. Press the clipped intersections open and the seam allowances toward the taupe squares. The block should measure 7¼" square, including the seam allowances. Repeat to make a total of 12 pieced B blocks.

Block B.
Make 12 blocks, 7¼" x 7¼".

Assembling the Quilt Top

1. Referring to the pictured quilt (page 38) and the quilt assembly diagram below, lay out the blocks in five horizontal rows, alternating the A and B blocks in each row and from row to row. Pin and then sew the blocks in each row together, matching the seam intersections. Clip the seam intersections. Press the clipped intersections open and the seam allowances toward the medium brown and taupe squares.

2. Join the rows. Clip the seam intersections and press as before. The pieced quilt center should measure 34¼" square, including the seam allowances.

3. Sew the red 3¾" × 34¼" border strips to the right and left sides of the quilt top. Press the seam allowances toward the border. Join the red 3¾" × 40¾" border strips to the remaining sides of the quilt center. Press the seam allowances toward the border.

Completing the Quilt

Layer and baste the quilt top, batting, and backing. Quilt the layers. The featured quilt was quilted by machine. Referring to "Jo's Single-Fold Binding" (page 126), or substituting your favorite method, join the tan strips into one length and use it to bind the quilt.

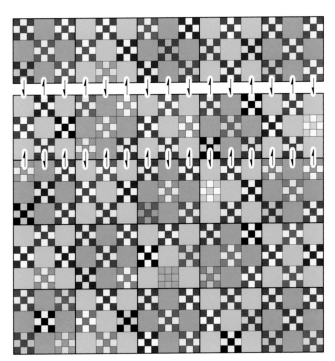

Quilt assembly

With its undeniable charm and versatility, the classic Nine Patch block has been favored by generations of quiltmakers. Endless setting and size options allow this block to be used in the humblest of quilts, or it can be "dressed to the nines" to steal the spotlight. ~ Kim

Swap Talk

This block exchange includes Nine Patch blocks stitched from light prints and an array of prints in richly hued autumn colors. Using two Nine Patch styles—half with dark corners and half with light corners—makes this block swap twice the fun!

Materials

Yardage is based on 42" of usable fabric width after prewashing and removing selvages. Fat quarters are 18" × 21" and chubby sixteenths are 9" × 10½".

44 squares, 5" × 5" *each*, of assorted dark prints in autumn colors for Nine Patch blocks

44 squares, 5" × 5" *each*, of assorted light prints for Nine Patch blocks

⅞ yard of coordinating light print for appliqué blocks and sashing

½ yard of black print for mini nine-patch units and binding

¼ yard (not a fat quarter) of light brown print for sashing

1 fat quarter of medium brown print for swag appliqués

2 chubby sixteenths of different red prints for oak-leaf appliqués

1 chubby sixteenth of orange print for oak-leaf appliqués

1 chubby sixteenth of gold print for oak-leaf appliqués

3 chubby sixteenths of assorted green prints for small-leaf appliqués

2⅝ yards of fabric for backing

46" × 46" square of batting

Supplies for your favorite traditional appliqué method

Finished quilt size:
39½" × 39½"

Finished exchange block size: 3" × 3"

Designed by Kim Diehl. Pieced by Connie Tabor and Kim Diehl. Machine appliquéd by Kim Diehl. Machine quilted by Karen Brown.

Cutting

You'll need 44 of each of the 2 styles of Nine Patch blocks (88 blocks total) to complete the featured quilt. For ease in piecing the blocks, keep the pieces for each block together as you cut them.

CUTTING FOR 1 DARK-CORNER AND 1 LIGHT-CORNER NINE PATCH BLOCK

From 1 dark print 5" square, cut:
9 squares, 1½" × 1½"

From 1 light print 5" square, cut:
9 squares, 1½" × 1½"

ADDITIONAL CUTTING

Cut all pieces across the width of the fabric in the order given unless otherwise noted. Cutting instructions for the appliqué pieces are provided separately.

From the coordinating light print, cut:
2 strips, 1½" × 42"
2 strips, 1" × 42"; crosscut *1 strip* in half to make
    2 strips, 1" × 21"
4 strips, 4¼" × 42"; crosscut into:
    8 rectangles, 4¼" × 12½"
    8 rectangles, 4¼" × 5"
1 strip, 2" × 42"; crosscut into 16 squares, 2" × 2"
5 squares, 1½" × 1½"

From the black print, cut:

5 binding strips, 2½" × 42" (see "Completing the Quilt" on page 49)

2 strips, 1" × 42"

1 strip, 1" × 21"

From the light brown print, cut:

5 strips, 1½" × 42"; crosscut *1 strip* into 4 squares, 1½" × 1½"

Piecing for Two Nine Patch Blocks

The instructions that follow will make one Nine Patch block with dark corners and one with light corners. Use the pieces cut for one pair of blocks and repeat as often as needed to make the required number of blocks. Sew all pieces with right sides together using a ¼" seam allowance unless otherwise noted. Press the seam allowances as indicated by the arrows or as otherwise specified.

1. To make the dark-corner Nine Patch block, lay out five dark 1½" squares and four light 1½" squares in three horizontal rows. Join the pieces in each row; press. Join the rows; press. The block should measure 3½" square, including the seam allowances.

Make 1 block, 3½" x 3½".

2. To make the light-corner Nine Patch block, lay out four dark 1½" squares and five light 1½" squares in three horizontal rows. Join the pieces in each row; press. Join the rows; press. The pieced block should measure 3½" square, including the seam allowances.

Make 1 block, 3½" x 3½".

3. Repeat steps 1 and 2 to make 88 Nine Patch blocks (44 of each).

Correcting Inaccurate Patchwork

Experience has taught me that when you participate in block swaps, there will be times when you receive blocks that aren't accurate in size . . . it just happens! Before tossing these onto the scrap heap, it's worth trying to turn lemons into lemonade and attempt corrections. For blocks that are too large, try giving them a generous misting of Best Press (or, as an alternative, set your iron to the steam setting), and then press the block to help shrink the fabric. Once the block has cooled, use your rotary cutter and acrylic ruler to square it up and trim away any excess seam allowance.

For blocks that are too small, set your iron to a hot, dry setting. Position a block right side up on your pressing board, and brace one side edge with your hand. Beginning at the center of the block, gently but firmly smooth the iron toward the outer edge. Rotate and repeat with each remaining side of the block. This little trick can help relax and stretch the fibers of the cloth slightly, and it's often enabled me to salvage what would otherwise be an unusable block. ~ Kim

Piecing the Mini Nine-Patch Units

1. Using the 1" × 42" strips, join a black strip to each long edge of a coordinating light strip to make strip set A; press. Crosscut the strip set into 40 segments, 1" wide.

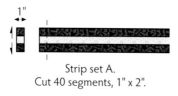

Strip set A.
Cut 40 segments, 1" x 2".

2. Using the 1" × 21" strips, join a coordinating light strip to each long edge of a black strip to make strip set B; press. Crosscut the strip set into 20 segments, 1" wide.

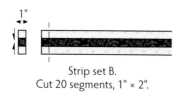

Strip set B.
Cut 20 segments, 1" x 2".

3. Sew an A segment to each long edge of a B segment; press. Repeat to make a total of 20 mini nine-patch units measuring 2" square, including the seam allowances.

Make 20 units,
2" x 2".

Assembling the Appliqué Backgrounds

1. Lay out five mini nine-patch units and four coordinating light 2" squares in three horizontal rows. Join the pieces in each row; press. Join the rows; press. Repeat to make a total of four double nine-patch units measuring 5" square, including the seam allowances.

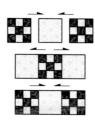

Make 4 units, 5" x 5".

2. Join light 4¼" × 5" rectangles to the right and left sides of a double nine-patch unit; press. Join light 4¼" × 12½" rectangles to the remaining sides of the unit; press. Repeat to make a total of four appliqué block backgrounds measuring 12½" square, including the seam allowances.

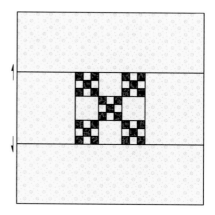

Make 4 blocks, 12½" x 12½".

Appliquéing the Blocks

The appliqué patterns are provided on page 49. Refer to "Kim's Invisible Machine-Appliqué Technique" on page 116 or use your favorite method.

1. Cut and prepare the following appliqués:
   - 16 swags from medium brown print
   - 4 oak leaves from *each* of the two red chubby sixteenths, the orange chubby sixteenth, and the gold chubby sixteenth (combined total of 16)
   - 32 small leaves *total* from the three assorted green chubby sixteenths

2. With right sides together, fold an appliqué block foundation in half lengthwise; use a hot, dry iron to lightly press a center crease. Open the block, and then continue folding and pressing to add a horizontal crease and two diagonal creases.

3. Referring to the pictured quilt, fold four swags in half to find the centers, and lightly finger-press the creases. Position a swag onto each side of the center double nine-patch unit, with the tips resting against the seams of the unit; pin or baste. Appliqué the swags in place.

4. Referring to the photo on page 44 for color placement, position the colors randomly on each corner of the block, lay out two red oak leaves, one orange oak leaf, and one gold oak leaf, with the inner points resting between the swags and the tips centered over the diagonal block creases; pin or baste. Appliqué the leaves in place.

5. Position, baste, and appliqué two small leaves along the curved outer edge of each swag.

6. Repeat steps 2–5 to complete four appliqué blocks measuring 12½" square, including the seam allowances.

Assembling the Quilt Top

1. Join light brown 1½" × 42" strips to both long sides of a coordinating light 1½" × 42" strip to make a pieced strip set C; press. Repeat for a total of two strip sets. Crosscut the strip sets into four segments, 12½" wide, for the pieced sashing strips.

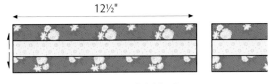

12½"

Strip set C. Make 2.
Cut 4 segments, 3½" x 12½".

2. Referring to "Piecing for Two Nine Patch Blocks" (page 45), use the five coordinating light 1½" squares and the four light brown 1½" squares to make a nine-patch unit with light corners measuring 3½" square, including the seam allowances.

3. Lay out the appliquéd blocks, the pieced sashing strips, and the nine-patch unit in three horizontal rows. Join the pieces in each row; press. Join the rows; press. The quilt center should measure 27½" square, including the seam allowances.

Adding the Nine Patch Border

1. Lay out five light-corner Nine Patch blocks and four dark-corner Nine Patch blocks in alternating positions. Join the blocks; press. Repeat to make a total of two short A border strips measuring 3½" × 27½", including the seam allowances.

Border A.
Make 2.

2. Repeat step 1 using five dark-corner Nine Patch blocks and four light-corner Nine Patch blocks, reversing the block placement, to make two short B border strips.

Border B.
Make 2.

3. Join a short A border strip to a short B border strip; press. Repeat to make two short border strips measuring 6½" × 27½", including the seam allowances. Using the pictured quilt as a guide, join the strip A edges to the right and left sides of the quilt center. Press the seam allowances toward the border.

Side borders.
Make 2.

Blending Block Colors

Because color guidelines are somewhat subjective and can be open to interpretation, it's possible to receive blocks with colors that are slightly off and don't blend well with the others. I've always loved that these blocks lend a bit of a "make-do" quality and I often intentionally add them to my quilts, but the key to using them successfully is in their placement. For any block that's obviously different from the others, I'll seek out a second block from the group that's the most similar and position the two of them side by side; the similar block will act as a "bridge" and minimize the differences. For blocks that are really prominent because of their colors or prints (I call these "zingers"), I've learned to place them in approximately opposite positions when I'm laying out the components of the quilt top (or space them at equal intervals around the quilt top if there are several). This approach will give the quilt a little bit of sparkle, while also lending a sense of balance, and the block choices will look intentional. Simple tricks, but very effective! ~ Kim

4. Repeat step 1 using seven light-corner Nine Patch blocks and six dark-corner Nine Patch blocks to make two long A border strips measuring 3½" × 39½", including the seam allowances. In the same manner, use seven dark-corner Nine Patch blocks and six light-corner Nine Patch blocks, reversing the block placement, to make two long B border strips.

5. Join a long A border strip to a long B border strip. Press the seam allowances toward border B. Repeat to make two pieced long border strips measuring 6½" × 39½", including the seam allowances. Using the pictured quilt as a guide, join the strip A edges to the remaining sides of the quilt center. Press the seam allowances toward the border.

Completing the Quilt

Layer and baste the quilt top, batting, and backing. Quilt the layers. The blocks of the featured quilt were machine quilted with small feathered wreaths around the center portion of the double nine-patch units, the appliqués were outlined to emphasize their shapes, and a small-scale stipple design was used to fill the open background areas. Xs were stitched onto the border Nine Patch blocks, with feathered vines radiating out from the center-most Nine Patch along the center sashing strips. Referring to "Kim's Chubby Binding" on page 127, or substituting your favorite method, use the black binding strips to bind the quilt.

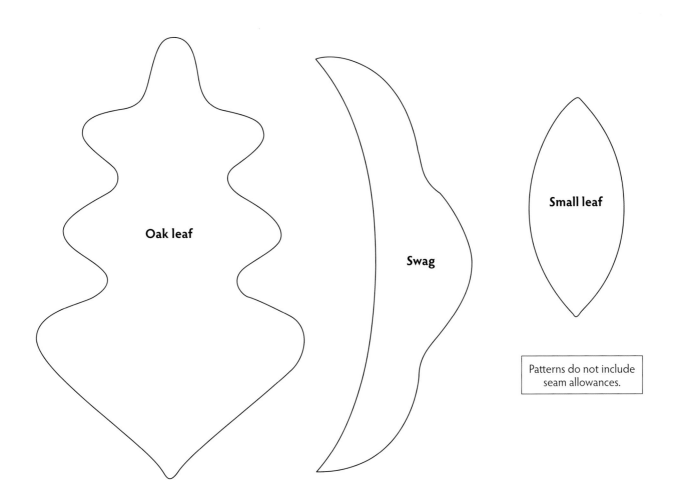

Oak leaf

Swag

Small leaf

Patterns do not include seam allowances.

Striking patchwork blocks stitched from a myriad of richly hued cream and indigo prints create a sense of movement and sparkle in this sweet little quilt. For even more options, try substituting your own favorite color, or raid your stash for a bit of scrappy charm. ~ Kim

Swap Talk

For this Yankee Puzzle block exchange, I chose a color scheme of indigo and cream, but any two colors with a good amount of contrast will work beautifully to achieve the bold geometric pattern featured in this quilt. The hourglass block units will be made in matching sets of four and then used to make the larger Yankee Puzzle block.

Materials

Yardage is based on 42" of usable fabric width after prewashing and removing selvages.

24 rectangles, 4" × 7" *each*, of assorted indigo prints for Yankee Puzzle blocks

24 rectangles, 4" × 7" *each*, of assorted cream prints for Yankee Puzzle blocks

¾ yard of coordinating indigo print for setting blocks, border, and binding

¼ yard (not a fat quarter) of coordinating cream print for setting blocks

1 yard of fabric for backing

33" × 33" square of batting

Cutting

You'll need 24 Yankee Puzzle blocks to complete this quilt. For ease in piecing the blocks, keep the pieces for each set of four hourglass units grouped together as you cut them.

CUTTING FOR 1 BLOCK

From 1 indigo print 4" × 7" rectangle, cut:
2 squares, 3¼" × 3¼"; cut each square in half diagonally *once* to yield 2 triangles (combined total of 4)

From 1 cream print 4" × 7" rectangle, cut:
2 squares, 3¼" × 3¼"; cut each square in half diagonally *once* to yield 2 triangles (combined total of 4)

Continued on page 52

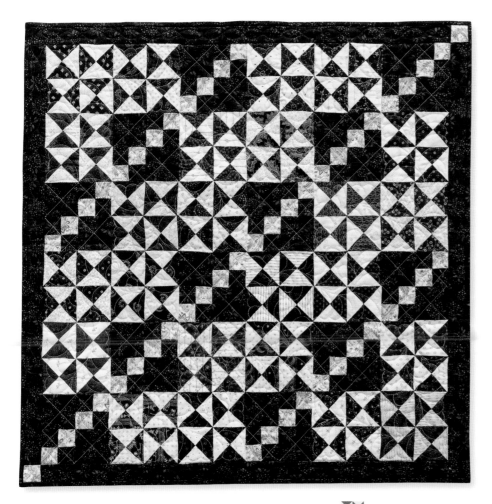

Finished quilt size:
26½" × 26½"

**Finished exchange
block size:** 4" × 4"

*Designed by Kim Diehl.
Pieced by Barbara Walsh
and Kim Diehl.
Machine quilted by
Karen Brown.*

Continued from page 50

ADDITIONAL CUTTING

*Cut all pieces across the width of the fabric in the order
given unless otherwise noted.*

From the coordinating indigo print, cut:

5 strips, 2½" × 42"; crosscut *2 of the strips* into
   24 squares, 2½" × 2½"
6 strips, 1½" × 42"; crosscut *4 of the strips* into:
   2 strips, 1½" × 24½"
   2 strips, 1½" × 25½"

From the coordinating cream print, cut:

2 strips, 1½" × 42"
2 squares, 1½" × 1½"

Piecing for One
Yankee Puzzle Block

*The instructions that follow will make one block.
Use the pieces cut for one block and repeat as many
times as needed to make the required number of
blocks. Sew all pieces with right sides together using
a ¼" seam allowance unless otherwise specified. Press the
seam allowances as indicated by the arrows or as
otherwise specified.*

1. Join an indigo triangle and a cream triangle
   along the long diagonal edges to make a half-
   square-triangle unit; press. Trim away the
   dog-ear points. Repeat to make a total of four

units measuring 2⅞" square, including the seam allowances.

Make 4 units,
2⅞" x 2⅞".

2. Using a rotary cutter and an acrylic ruler, cut each pieced half-square-triangle unit in half diagonally through the sewn seam to yield eight pieced triangles.

Make 8.

3. Join the pieced triangles along long diagonal edges as shown, positioning the units so the light and dark prints oppose each other; press. Trim away the dog-ear points. Repeat to make a total of four hourglass units measuring 2½" square, including the seam allowances.

Make 4 units, 2½" x 2½".

4. Lay out the hourglass units in two horizontal rows of two units each. Join the units in each row; press. Join the rows; press. The pieced block should measure 4½" square, including the seam allowances.

Yankee Puzzle block,
4½" x 4½".

5. Repeat steps 1–4 to make 24 Yankee Puzzle blocks.

Piecing the Setting Blocks

1. Join a coordinating indigo and a coordinating cream 1½" × 42" strip along the long edges to make a pieced strip set; press. Repeat for a total of two pieced strip sets. Crosscut the strip sets into 48 segments, 1½" wide.

Make 2 strip sets.
Cut 48 segments, 1½" x 2½".

2. Lay out two strip-set segments in two horizontal rows. Join the segments; press. Repeat to make a total of 24 four-patch units measuring 2½" square, including the seam allowances.

Make 24 units,
2½" x 2½".

3. Lay out two four-patch units and two indigo 2½" squares in two horizontal rows; press. Join the pieces in each row; press. Join the rows; press. Repeat to make a total of 12 pieced setting blocks measuring 4½" square, including the seam allowances.

Make 12 blocks, 4½" x 4½".

Assembling the Quilt Top

1. Lay out six Yankee Puzzle blocks and three setting blocks in three horizontal rows. Join the blocks in each row; press. Join the rows; press. Repeat to assemble a total of four block units measuring 12½" square, including the seam allowances.

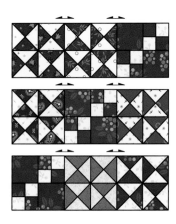

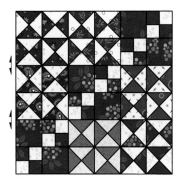

Make 4 units, 12½" x 12½".

2. Referring to the pictured quilt (page 52), lay out the four block units in two horizontal rows of two units each to form the quilt center. Join the units in each row. Press the seam allowances open. Join the rows. Press the seam allowances open. The quilt center should measure 24½" square, including the seam allowances.

Quilt assembly

3. Join indigo 1½" × 24½" border strips to the right and left sides of the quilt center. Press the seam allowances toward the border. Sew a cream 1½" square to one end of each indigo 1½" × 25½" border strip. Press the seam allowances toward the strips. Referring to the pictured quilt, join these strips to the top and bottom of the quilt center. Press the seam allowances toward the border. The quilt top should measure 26½" square, including the seam allowances.

Completing the Quilt

Layer and baste the quilt top, batting, and backing. Quilt the layers. The featured quilt was machine quilted with Xs stitched onto each quadrant of the setting blocks, a meandering feathered vine was stitched onto the diagonal Double X rows and a cable design was stitched onto the indigo portions of the border. Referring to "Kim's Chubby Binding" on page 127, or substituting your favorite method, use the remaining three indigo strips to bind the quilt.

Alternate Settings

To me, a quilt design is a bit like a recipe— a perfect jumping-off point as you work toward finishing your project, but nearly anything can be tweaked and changed to create an end result that's uniquely yours. My friend Barbara Walsh chose to make an alternate version of this quilt, with her block components rearranged into a different setting, and the results are spectacular. What a great reminder to explore the endless possibilities that each new project brings! ~ Kim

Parkersburg

Colorful Yankee Puzzle blocks made from alternating light and dark prints create an intricate sea of patchwork surrounding the star of the show, the center appliqué block. To give you an idea of scale, that center block is just 5¾" square! If you're new to appliqué, this is a great project for giving it a try. ~ Jo

Swap Talk

A quilt like this may look, or sound, daunting, what with 160 hourglass units needed to make the 40 blocks. But divvy up the task among friends and you can assembly-line piece those 2" units and swap them to get a great mix of fabrics and colors for this medallion quilt. Each participant chooses her desired color palette, and then makes blocks for each of the others in the group. In my swap, we had eight quilters, so each of us made eight sets of five blocks. Be sure to count yourself in the total number of quilters in the group so that you make a set of blocks for yourself too!

Materials

Yardage is based on 42" of usable fabric width after prewashing and removing selvages. Fat quarters are 18" × 21" and fat eighths are 9" × 21".

Approximately ⅞ yard *total* of assorted cream shirting prints for Yankee Puzzle blocks

Approximately ⅞ yard *total* of assorted dark prints in teals, browns, reds, and pinks for Yankee Puzzle blocks

7" × 7" square of light print for center unit appliqué background

6" × 6" square of teal print for oak-leaf appliqué

5" × 5" square of brown print for small-leaf appliqués

4" × 4" square of medium tan print for center unit inner-border cornerstones

1 fat eighth of brown stripe for appliqué unit corners

1 fat eighth *each* of a brown print and a light tan print for center unit inner border

1 fat quarter of red print for center unit outer border

1 yard of dark brown print for inner border

1¼ yards of brown floral stripe for outer border

¼ yard of red stripe for single-fold binding

2½ yards of fabric for backing

44" × 44" square of batting

Supplies for your favorite appliqué method

Finished quilt size:
37½" × 37½"

Finished exchange block size: 4" × 4"

Designed by Jo Morton. Pieced by Sheri Dowding, Mary Fornoff, Cindy Hansen, and Phyllis Masters. Machine quilted by Maggi Honeyman.

Cutting

You'll need 40 Yankee Puzzle blocks to complete the featured quilt. For ease in piecing the blocks, keep the pieces for each block grouped together as you cut them.

CUTTING FOR 1 BLOCK

From *each* of 2 different cream prints, cut:
1 square, 3¼" × 3¼" (combined total of 2)

From *each* of 2 different dark prints, cut:
1 square, 3¼" × 3¼" (combined total of 2)

ADDITIONAL CUTTING

Cut all pieces across the width of the fabric in the order given unless otherwise noted.

From the brown stripe, cut:
2 squares, 5¾" × 5¾"; cut 1 square in half diagonally from top right to lower left and cut 1 square in half diagonally from top left to lower right to yield a total of 4 triangles

From the light tan print, cut:
4 squares, 3¼" × 3¼"

From the brown print, cut:
16 squares, 1⅞" × 1⅞"

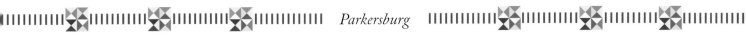
From the medium tan print, cut:
4 squares, 1½" × 1½"

From the *lengthwise grain* of the red print, cut:*
2 strips, 1½" × 10½"
2 strips, 1½" × 12½"

From the *lengthwise grain* of the dark brown print, cut:*
2 strips, 1" × 28½"
2 strips, 1" × 29½"

From the *lengthwise grain* of the brown floral stripe, fussy cut:*
2 strips, 4½" × 29½"
2 strips, 4½" × 37½"

From the red stripe, cut:
4 single-fold binding strips, 1⅛" × 42" (see "Completing the Quilt" on page 62)

*Jo recommends cutting these pieces on the lengthwise grain of the fabric (parallel to the selvage), because it has the least amount of stretch and will give you nice, straight edges.

Piecing for One Yankee Puzzle Block

The instructions that follow will make one block. Use the pieces cut for one block and repeat as many times as needed to make the required number of blocks, mixing and matching half-square-triangle units if you're making multiple blocks. Sew all pieces with right sides together using a scant ¼" seam allowance unless otherwise noted. Press the seam allowances as indicated by the arrows or as otherwise specified.

1. Use a pencil and an acrylic ruler to draw a diagonal sewing line from corner to corner on the wrong side of each light 3¼" square.

2. Place a marked light square on top of a dark 3¼" square, right sides together. Sew a scant ¼" from each side of the drawn line. Cut the squares apart on the drawn line to make two half-square-triangle units; press. Repeat for a

total of four half-square-triangle units. Each unit should measure 2⅞" square, including the seam allowances.

Make 4 units,
2⅞" x 2⅞".

3. Draw a diagonal line from corner to corner on the wrong side of two half-square-triangle units made of different prints, marking the line through the sewn seam. Place a marked unit on top of one of the remaining units, positioning the units so the light and dark prints oppose each other. Sew a scant ¼" from each side of the drawn line. Cut apart the units on the drawn line to make two hourglass units. Refer to "Jo's Clipping Trick" (page 114) to clip the seam intersections. Press the clipped intersections open and the seam allowances toward the darker prints. Repeat to make a total of four hourglass units measuring 2½" square, including the seam allowances.

Make 4 units,
2½" x 2½".

4. Lay out the hourglass units in two horizontal rows of two units each. Join the units in each row; press. Join the rows. Clip the seam intersection. Press the clipped intersection open and the seam allowances toward the darker print. The block should measure 4½" square, including the seam allowances.

Yankee Puzzle block,
4½" x 4½".

Appliquéing and Assembling the Center Unit

The appliqué patterns are provided on page 63. Jo achieves great appliqué results with her back-basting needle-turn technique (page 124), but you can use your own favorite method.

1. Fold the light 7" square in half diagonally in each direction and lightly finger-press the folds. Using your favorite appliqué technique, cut and prepare:
   - 1 oak leaf from the teal 6" square
   - 4 small leaves from the brown 5" square

2. Center and stitch the appliqué shapes to the light square using the crease marks for positioning. Square up the appliquéd unit to measure 6¼" square.

3. Sew brown stripe triangles to opposite sides of the appliquéd square, paying close attention to the direction of the stripe. Press. Repeat on the remaining sides of the square; press. Square up the unit to measure 8½" square.

Appliqué block,
8½" x 8½".

4. Using the brown print 1⅞" squares and the light tan 3¼" squares, refer to "Jo's No-Waste Flying-Geese Method" (page 115) to make 16 flying-geese units. Each unit should measure 1½" × 2½", including the seam allowances.

5. Join four flying-geese units side by side to make a center unit pieced inner-border strip; press. The strip should measure 1½" × 8½", including the seam allowances. Repeat for a total of four pieced inner-border strips.

Make 4 units, 1½" x 8½".

6. Referring to the center-unit assembly diagram on page 61, pin and then sew pieced inner-border strips to the right and left sides of the appliquéd block, with the tan edges toward the block edges.

7. Join a medium tan 1½" square to each end of the remaining two pieced inner-border strips. Press the seam allowances toward the squares. Pin and then sew these strips to the remaining sides of the center unit, matching seam intersections. Clip the seam intersections at the cornerstones. Press the clipped intersections open and the seam allowances toward the squares and center. The center unit should now measure 10½" square, including the seam allowances.

8. Join the red 1½" × 10½" center unit border strips to the right and left sides of the center unit. Press. Add the red 1½" × 12½" center unit border strips to the remaining sides of the center unit. Press. The center unit should

measure 12½" square, including the seam allowances.

Center-unit assembly

No Fudging on Medallions!

Because the center block is surrounded by a pieced border and then additional patchwork, there's really no room for fudging. So make sure your center unit measures exactly 12½" square before you begin adding the Yankee Puzzle blocks. If your unit is too big or too small, you can adjust the red border as needed by sewing a narrower or deeper seam (same amount on all sides!). ~ Jo

Staying Organized

Pin a note to the top-left section of the quilt center indicating which edge is the top, and then return the section to the design wall. That way, you can be sure when you sew the next section that you have the blocks positioned exactly as you'd laid them out. Step back and look at each section before proceeding, so you can catch any needed changes before you get too far along. ~ Jo

Assembling the Quilt Top

1. Referring to the quilt assembly diagram on page 62, arrange the Yankee Puzzle blocks on your design wall in two horizontal rows of seven blocks each for the top third of the quilt.

2. Sew the first two blocks in each row together. Press the seam allowances open. Sew the joined blocks together to make the top-left section. Press the seam allowances open. Repeat with the last two blocks in each row to make the top-right section. In the same manner, join the blocks in the middle of each row, and then join the rows to make the top-middle section. Join the sections to complete the top section of the quilt center. Place the section back on the design wall.

3. Repeat steps 1 and 2 to make the bottom section of the quilt center.

4. Place the appliquéd center unit between the top and bottom sections on the design wall. Lay out the remaining Yankee Puzzle blocks in three horizontal rows of two blocks each on each side of the center unit. Join the blocks in each row. Press the seam allowances open. Join the rows on each side of the center unit. Press the seam allowances open. Join the block units to the sides of the center unit to complete the center section. Press the seam allowances toward the center unit.

5. Join the top and bottom sections to the center section. Press the seam allowances open. The pieced quilt top should measure 28½" square, including the seam allowances.

6. Sew the dark brown 1" × 28½" inner-border strips to the right and left sides of the quilt top. Press the seam allowances toward the border. Join the 1" × 29½" inner-border strips to the remaining sides of the quilt top. Press the seam allowances toward the border. The pieced quilt top should measure 29½" square, including the seam allowances.

7. Join the floral 4½" × 29½" outer-border strips to the right and left sides of the quilt top. Press the seam allowances toward the outer border. Add the floral 37½"-long border strips to the remaining sides of the quilt top. Press the seam allowances toward the outer border.

Completing the Quilt

Layer and baste the quilt top, batting, and backing. Quilt the layers. The featured quilt was quilted by machine. Referring to "Jo's Single-Fold Binding" (page 126), or substituting your favorite method, join the red stripe strips into one length and use it to bind the quilt.

Quilt assembly

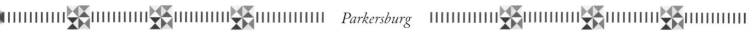

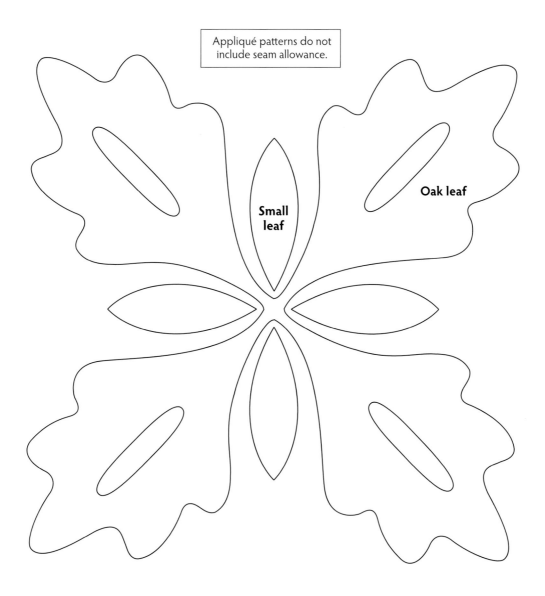

Appliqué patterns do not include seam allowance.

Small leaf

Oak leaf

Berry Baskets

Commonly, Basket blocks are constructed with darker fabrics for the baskets and lighter values for the backgrounds. For these charming little baskets—they're just 4" finished!—I asked my friends to switch things up, so the basket tops are stitched from cream shirting prints, while the backgrounds are rich browns. The basket bottoms are tans and lighter browns. Just make sure your fabrics have enough contrast so that the baskets don't disappear completely into the background. ~ Jo

Swap Talk

Berry Baskets is a fun project for a smaller group of quilting friends. I made this with three other participants. We each created 4 blocks for a total of 16. I chose an earthy palette of rich browns, tans, and taupes and set them off with a pink print. Each friend can choose her own color palette, making it fun to compare the finished quilts. If your friends are fearful of small half-square-triangle units (they measure just 1½" square), see my tip on page 67 for using triangle paper to achieve precise results.

Materials

Yardage is based on 42" of usable fabric width after prewashing and removing selvages.

Approximately ¼ yard *total* of assorted cream shirting prints for basket tops

Approximately ⅝ yard *total* of assorted dark brown prints for basket backgrounds

Approximately ⅓ yard *total* of assorted medium tan prints for basket bottoms

⅝ yard of pink print for setting pieces

⅞ yard of floral stripe for inner border

1 yard of brown stripe for outer border

¼ yard of brown-and-pink stripe for single-fold binding

1¼ yards of fabric for backing

38" × 38" square of batting

Cutting

You'll need 16 Basket blocks to complete the featured quilt. For ease in piecing the blocks, keep the pieces for each block grouped together as you cut them.

CUTTING FOR 1 BASKET BLOCK

From the assorted cream shirting prints, cut a *total* of:
3 squares, 2" × 2"

From the assorted dark brown prints, cut a *total* of:
3 squares, 2" × 2"
1 square, 1⅞" × 1⅞"; cut in half diagonally *once* to yield 2 small triangles

Continued on page 66

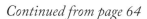

**Finished quilt
size:** 31⅛" × 31⅛"

**Finished
exchange block
size:** 4" × 4"

*Designed by
Jo Morton. Pieced
by Sheri Dowding,
Mary Fornoff,
Cindy Hansen, and
Phyllis Masters.
Machine quilted by
Maggi Honeyman.*

Continued from page 64

From 1 dark brown print, cut:

1 square, 2⅞" × 2⅞"; cut in half diagonally
once to yield 2 large triangles. (You'll use 1
triangle and have 1 left over for another block
if desired. If you use the leftover triangle for
another block, be sure to cut 2 additional
matching 1½" × 2½" rectangles.)

2 rectangles, 1½" × 2½"

From 1 medium tan print, cut:

1 square, 2⅞" × 2⅞"; cut in half diagonally
once to yield 2 large triangles. (You'll use 1
triangle and have 1 left over for another block
if desired. If you use the leftover triangle for
another block, be sure to cut 1 additional
matching 1⅞" square.)

1 square, 1⅞" × 1⅞"; cut in half diagonally *once* to
yield 2 small triangles

66

ADDITIONAL CUTTING

Cut all pieces across the width of the fabric in the order given unless otherwise noted.

From the pink print, cut:
3 squares, 7¼" × 7¼"; cut each square in half
    diagonally *twice* to yield 4 side setting triangles
    (combined total of 12)
9 squares, 4½" × 4½"
2 squares, 4" × 4"; cut each square in half
    diagonally *once* to yield 2 corner setting
    triangles (combined total of 4)

From the *lengthwise grain* of the floral stripe, fussy cut:*
2 strips, 1½" × 23⅛"
2 strips, 1½" × 25⅛"

From the *lengthwise grain* of the brown stripe, cut:*
2 strips, 3½" × 25⅛"
2 strips, 3½" × 31⅛"

From the brown-and-pink stripe, cut:
4 single-fold binding strips, 1⅛" × 42" (see
    "Completing the Quilt" on page 69)

*Jo recommends cutting these pieces on the lengthwise grain of the fabric (parallel to the selvage), because it has the least amount of stretch and will give you nice, straight edges.

Piecing for One Basket Block

The instructions that follow will make one block. Use the pieces cut for one block and repeat as many times as needed to make the required number of blocks. Sew all pieces with right sides together using a scant ¼" seam allowance unless otherwise noted. Press the seam allowances as indicated by the arrows or as otherwise specified.

1. Draw a diagonal sewing line from corner to
   corner on the wrong side of each cream 2"
   square. Place a marked light print square on
   top of a dark brown 2" square, right sides
   together. Sew a scant ¼" from each side of
   the drawn line. Cut the squares apart on the
   drawn line to make two half-square-triangle
   units; press. Repeat for a total of six half-
   square-triangle units. Square up each unit to
   1½" square, including the seam allowances.

Make 6 units,
1½" × 1½".

Using Half-Square-Triangle Paper

There are several products available specifically for making half-square-triangle units. These foundation papers already have the lines marked on them, so all you need to do is layer your two fabric squares right sides together, place the paper on top, and sew on the marked lines. The paper stabilizes the pieces, so your units are accurate every time—there's no need to square them up. These papers are especially great to use when you have lots of units to make. For this project, I cut my triangle paper two units wide by two units high and made eight identical half-square-triangle units at a time. ~ Jo

2. Arrange the six half-square-triangle units and the dark brown small triangles in three horizontal rows. Sew the pieces in each row together; press. Pin and then sew the rows together, matching the seam intersections. Refer to "Jo's Clipping Trick" (page 114) to clip the seam intersections. Press the clipped intersections open and the seam allowances toward the dark brown triangles.

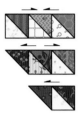

3. Center and sew the medium tan large triangle on the angled edge of the step 2 unit; press. Square up the unit to measure 3½" square, including the seam allowances.

4. Join the medium tan small triangles to the ends of the dark brown 1½" × 2½" rectangles as shown to make the basket feet units; press.

5. Sew the basket feet units to the left and bottom edges of the step 3 unit; press.

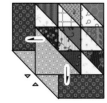

6. Sew the dark brown large triangle to the angled edge of the basket base to complete the block; press. Square up the block to measure 4½" square, including the seam allowances.

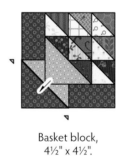

Basket block,
4½" x 4½".

7. Repeat steps 1–6 to make 16 Basket blocks.

Assembling the Quilt Top

1. Referring to the quilt assembly diagram on page 69, lay out the blocks, the pink 4½" squares, and the pink side setting triangles in diagonal rows. Join the pieces in each row; press. Pin and then sew the rows together, matching the seam intersections. Clip the seam intersections. Press the clipped intersections open and the seam allowances

toward the pink print. Add the pink corner setting triangles to each corner. Press the seam allowances toward the triangles.

2. Carefully trim the quilt-top edges ¼" from the block points, squaring up the pieced quilt top to measure 23⅛" square, including the seam allowances.

3. Sew the floral 1½" × 23⅛" inner-border strips to the right and left sides of the quilt top; press the seam allowances toward the borders. Join the floral 1½" × 25⅛" inner-border strips to the remaining sides of the quilt top; press the seam allowances toward the borders. The pieced quilt top should measure 25⅛" square, including the seam allowances.

4. Sew the brown stripe 3½" × 25⅛" outer-border strips to the right and left sides of the quilt top; press the seam allowances toward the borders. Join the brown stripe 3½" × 31⅛" outer-border strips to the remaining sides of the quilt top; press the seam allowances toward the borders.

Completing the Quilt

Layer and baste the quilt top, batting, and backing. Quilt the layers. The featured quilt was quilted by machine. Referring to "Jo's Single-Fold Binding" (page 126), or substituting your favorite method, join the brown-and-pink strips into one length and use it to bind the quilt.

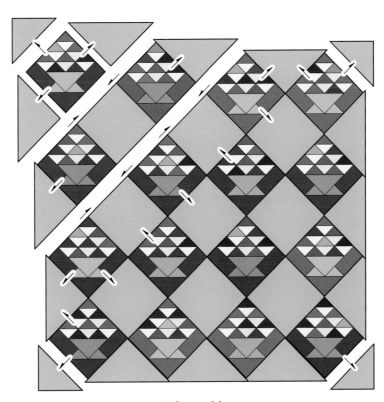

Quilt assembly

Cake in the Cabin

Break out your favorite black and red prints, and throw your own personal patchwork party as you stitch them into these tasty Cake Stand blocks. Log Cabin–style strips and a sparkling sawtooth border are the icing on this sweet little quilt cake. ~ Kim

Swap Talk

With a simple rotation to the direction of the pieced half-square-triangle units that form the top of a traditional Basket block, it's easy to create the Cake Stand block used in this quilt. Richly hued black, red, and tan prints are ideal for the bold geometric style of this quilt.

Materials

Yardage is based on 42" of usable fabric width after prewashing and removing selvages. Fat quarters are 18" × 21" and chubby sixteenths are 9" × 10½".

36 squares, 8" × 8" *each*, of assorted tan prints for block backgrounds and block sashing strips

36 rectangles, 3" × 5" *each*, of assorted red prints for cake-stand tops

36 rectangles, 4" × 7" *each*, of assorted black prints for cake-stand bases

3 chubby sixteenths of coordinating tan prints for setting patchwork

½ yard of tan print A for block sashing and outer border

½ yard of coordinating red print for block sashing and outer border

⅝ yard of coordinating black print for sashing, inner border, and binding

1 fat quarter of tan print B for quilt center sashing and outer-border cornerstones

1¼ yards of fabric for backing

41" × 41" square of batting

Finished quilt size: 34½" × 34½"

Finished exchange block size: 4" × 4"

Designed by Kim Diehl. Pieced by Jennifer Martinez and Kim Diehl. Machine quilted by Karen Brown.

Cutting

You'll need 36 Cake Stand blocks to complete the featured quilt. For ease in piecing the blocks, keep the pieces for each block grouped together as you cut them.

CUTTING FOR 1 CAKE STAND BLOCK

From 1 tan print 8" square, cut:

1 square, 2⅞" × 2⅞"; cut in half diagonally *once* to yield 2 triangles (you'll use 1 triangle and have 1 left over)

1 square, 2½" × 2½"

2 squares, 1⅞" × 1⅞"; cut each square in half diagonally *once* to yield 2 triangles (combined total of 4)

2 rectangles, 1½" × 2½"

1 square, 1½" × 1½"

From 1 red print 3" × 5" rectangle, cut:

2 squares, 1⅞" × 1⅞"; cut each square in half diagonally *once* to yield 2 triangles (combined total of 4)

From 1 black print 4" × 7" rectangle, cut:

1 square, 2⅞" × 2⅞"; cut in half diagonally *once* to yield 2 triangles (you'll use 1 triangle and have 1 left over for another project)

2 squares, 1½" × 1½"

ADDITIONAL CUTTING

Cut all pieces across the width of the fabric in the order given unless otherwise noted.

From *each* of the 3 coordinating tan prints, cut:
9 rectangles, 1½" × 3½" (combined total of 27)

From tan print A, cut:
1 strip, 1½" × 42"; crosscut into 9 rectangles,
    1½" × 3½"
3 strips, 2½" × 42"; crosscut into 24 rectangles,
    2½" × 3½"
1 strip, 2⅞" × 42"; crosscut into 12 squares,
    2⅞" × 2⅞". Cut each square in half diagonally
    once to yield 2 triangles (combined total of 24).

From the coordinating red print, cut:
3 strips, 1½" × 42"; crosscut into 60 squares,
    1½" × 1½"
2 strips, 2½" × 42"; crosscut into 24 squares,
    2½" × 2½"
1 strip, 2⅞" × 42"; crosscut into 12 squares,
    2⅞" × 2⅞". Cut each square in half diagonally
    once to yield 24 triangles.

From the coordinating black print, cut:
4 binding strips, 2½" × 42" (see "Completing the
    Quilt" on page 77)
1 strip, 1½" × 42"; crosscut into 13 squares,
    1½" × 1½"
4 strips, 1" × 42"; crosscut into:
    2 strips, 1" × 29½"
    2 strips, 1" × 30½"

From tan print B, cut:
4 squares, 2½" × 2½"
12 strips, 1½" × 9½"

Piecing for One Cake Stand Block

The instructions that follow will make one block. Use the pieces cut for one block and repeat as many times as needed to make the required number of blocks. Sew all pieces with right sides together using a ¼" seam allowance unless otherwise noted. Press the seam allowances as indicated by the arrows or as otherwise specified.

1. Join a red print and a tan print 1⅞" triangle along the long diagonal edges to make a half-square-triangle unit; press. Trim away the dog-ear points. Repeat to make a total of four half-square-triangle units measuring 1½" square, including the seam allowances.

Make 4 units,
1½" x 1½".

2. Join two half-square-triangle units to make a side unit; press. Repeat to make a mirror-image side unit.

Make 1 of each, 1½" x 2½".

3. Join, press, and trim a black print and a tan print 2⅞" triangle as instructed in step 1 to make a cake-stand base unit.

Make 1,
2½" x 2½".

4. Join the side unit to the top edge of the cake-stand base unit; press. Join a tan print 1½" square to the red end of the mirror-image side unit; press. Join this unit to the left-hand edge of the basket-base unit. The unit should measure 3½" square.

  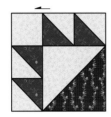

Make 1,
3½" x 3½".

5. Join a black 1½" square to the end of a tan 1½" × 2½" rectangle; press. Repeat to make a total of two pieced rectangles that are 1½" × 3½".

Make 2, 1½" x 3½".

6. Join a pieced rectangle to the bottom and right edges of the step 4 unit; press.

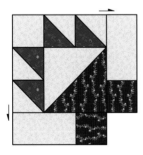

7. Using a pencil and an acrylic ruler, draw a diagonal sewing line from corner to corner on the wrong side of the tan print 2½" square. Layer the prepared square onto the open corner beneath the pieced basket base,

aligning the raw edges for perfect positioning. Stitch the square to the block unit along the drawn line. Fold the resulting inner triangle open to form the Cake Stand block corner; press. Trim away the layers beneath the top triangle, leaving a ¼" seam allowance. The Cake Stand block should measure 4½" square, including the seam allowances.

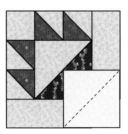 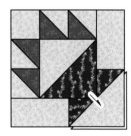

Cake Stand block,
4½" x 4½".

8. Repeat steps 1–7 to make 36 Cake Stand blocks.

Assembling the Quilt Top

1. Select one 1½" × 3½" rectangle from *each* of the three coordinating tan prints and tan print A. Join a red 1½" square to one end of each tan rectangle. Press the seam allowances toward the red print.

2. Lay out four pieced Cake Stand blocks, four pieced rectangles from step 1, and one black print 1½" square in three horizontal rows. Join the pieces in each row; press. Join the rows; press. Repeat to make a total of nine sashed block units measuring 9½" square, including the seam allowances.

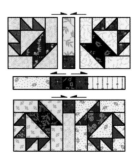 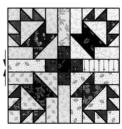

Make 9 units,
9½" x 9½".

74

3. Lay out three block units from step 2 and two tan B 1½" × 9½" sashing strips in alternating positions. Join the pieces; press. Repeat to make a total of three block rows measuring 9½" × 29½", including the seam allowances.

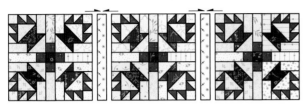

Make 3 rows,
9½" x 29½".

4. Lay out three tan B 1½" × 9½" sashing strips and two black 1½" squares in alternating positions. Join the pieces; press. Repeat to make a total of two sashing rows measuring 1½" × 29½", including the seam allowances.

Make 2 rows, 1½" x 29½".

5. Referring to the pictured quilt (page 72), lay out the block and sashing rows in alternating positions. Join the rows. Press the seam allowances toward the sashing rows. The pieced quilt top should measure 29½" square, including the seam allowances.

Adding the Borders

1. Join a black 1" × 29½" inner-border strip to the right and left sides of the quilt center. Press the seam allowances toward the border. Join black 1" × 30½" inner-border strips to the remaining sides of the quilt center. Press the seam allowances toward the border.

2. Using a pencil and an acrylic ruler, draw a diagonal sewing line from corner to corner on the wrong side of each red print 2½" square and each of the 24 remaining red print 1½" squares.

3. Layer a prepared red 2½" square onto one end of a tan print A 2½" × 3½" rectangle. Stitch the pair together along the drawn line. Fold the resulting inner triangle open, aligning the corner with the corner of the tan rectangle; press. Trim away the layers beneath the top triangle, leaving a ¼" seam allowance. Repeat to make a total of 12 pieced rectangles and 12 mirror-image rectangles. If desired, you can save the trimmed triangles to make the bonus mini-quilt on page 77.

Make 12 each.

4. Layer, stitch, press, and trim a prepared red 1½" square onto the bottom corner of each step 3 rectangle. Make sure to join these to the tan rectangle as shown.

Make 12 each.

5. Join a red print and a tan print A 2⅞" triangle to make a half-square-triangle unit as instructed in step 1 of "Piecing for One Cake Stand Block" (page 73). Repeat to make a total of 24 half-square-triangle units.

6. Lay out one step 4 unit, one mirror-image step 4 unit, and two half-square-triangle units as shown. Join the units; press. Repeat to make a total of 12 pieced border units measuring 2½" × 10½", including the seam allowances.

Make 12 units,
2½" x 10½".

7. Referring to the quilt assembly diagram below, join three pieced border units end to end. Press the seam allowances open. Repeat to make a total of four pieced border rows measuring 2½" × 30½", including the seam allowances.

8. Join pieced borders to the right and left sides of the quilt top. Press. Join a tan print B 2½" square to the end of each remaining pieced border row. Press. Join these strips to the remaining sides of the quilt top. Press. The quilt top should measure 34½" square, including the seam allowances.

Quilt assembly

Completing the Quilt

Layer and baste the quilt top, batting, and backing. Quilt the layers. The featured quilt was machine quilted with concentric arcs radiating out from the base of each Cake Stand block. Xs were stitched onto the red and black squares at the center of each block unit, with elongated Xs stitched onto the coordinating tan print rectangles and tan B sashing strips. The black inner border was stitched in the ditch (along the seamlines). The red triangles in the outer border were echo quilted ¼" inside the seamlines. The tan background area was stippled, and the cornerstones each have an X. Referring to "Kim's Chubby Binding" on page 127, or substituting your favorite method, use the black binding strips to bind the quilt.

"Double-Dipped" Scraps

This Cake in the Cabin project presented a perfect opportunity for me to "double-dip" my trimmed flying-geese unit corner scraps and use them to stitch an adorable little bonus project.

First, I joined 20 pairs of layered triangles along the long diagonal edges and pressed them as directed in the quilt instructions, and then trimmed them to 1½" square. Next, I joined the half-square-triangle units to make five pinwheel units. I then used scraps to make four flying-geese setting units as instructed in step 3 of "Adding the Borders" (using a red print 1½" × 2½" rectangle and two tan print A 1½" squares for each unit), and then joined them to 1½" × 2½" rectangles. After piecing the quilt center, I stitched a tan B 2½" square to each end of a red 2½" × 6½" rectangle as previously instructed

to make four blunted flying-geese units, which I joined with red 2½" squares to form the border. Finished!
~ Kim

77

Warm Regards

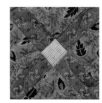 Gather a plethora of pretty prints, add a sprinkling of yo-yo berries and blooms, and what's the happy result? This vibrant quilted garden, brimming over with colorful blocks, blossoms, and birds in sun-drenched colors that will never fade. ~ Kim

Swap Talk

Block swaps are usually very structured when it comes to color schemes, but scrappy swaps are entirely doable with just a few simple guidelines. For this swap I opted to use prints in assorted colors for the X areas in the Old Italian blocks, choosing three prints per block in any combination that was pleasing. My color guidelines include rich, slightly muddy colors (nothing clear or bright—for instance, lemon yellow would be a "no" but gold would be ideal), and no white! It was great fun putting prints together for each block and being surprised at the results.

You can make this a double swap by sharing a 5" charm square from one or two of the prints in each block and use them to stitch the yo-yos. Did I mention this exchange is fun? Super fun!

Materials

Yardage is based on 42" of usable fabric width after prewashing and removing selvages. Fat quarters are 18" × 21", fat eighths are 9" × 21", chubby sixteenths are 9" × 10½", and charm squares are 5" × 5".

68 rectangles, 4" × 9" *each*, of assorted print scraps for Old Italian blocks

68 squares, 4¾" × 4¾" *each*, for Old Italian blocks

68 squares, 1½" × 1½" *each*, for Old Italian block centers

78 charm squares or 1⅝ yards *total* of assorted prints for yo-yos

2⅛ yards of tan print for appliqué blocks and border patchwork

½ yard of green print for stem and leaf appliqués

3 fat quarters of coordinating green prints for leaf appliqués

1 chubby sixteenth of dark blue print for bird appliqués

1 charm square of medium blue print for bird wing appliqués

Continued on page 80

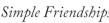

Finished quilt size:
60½" × 60½"

Finished exchange block size: 5" × 5"

Designed by Kim Diehl. Pieced by Jennifer Martinez and Kim Diehl. Machine quilted by Leisa Wiggley.

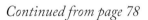

Continued from page 78

1 fat eighth of brown or black stripe or print for vase appliqués

1½ yards of red print for appliqués, border patchwork, and binding

1 charm square of cheddar or gold print for star appliqués

3¾ yards of fabric for backing

67" × 67" square of batting

Freezer paper

Bias bar to make ⅜" stems

Liquid glue for fabric, water-soluble and acid-free (Kim likes the results achieved with Quilter's Choice Basting Glue by Beacon Adhesives)

Clover small yo-yo maker

#12 or #8 perle cotton for stitching the yo-yos (Kim used Valdani's variegated #12 perle cotton in color H212 Faded Brown)

Size 5 embroidery needle

Supplies for your favorite traditional appliqué method

Cutting

You'll need 68 Old Italian blocks to complete the featured quilt. For ease in piecing the blocks, keep the rectangles for each block grouped together by print.

CUTTING FOR 1 OLD ITALIAN BLOCK

From *each* of the assorted print 4" × 9" rectangles, cut:

4 rectangles, 1½" × 4" (272 total)

Please refer to the "Using Directional Prints" tip (page 82) if you're using directional print fabric.

ADDITIONAL CUTTING

Cut all pieces across the width of the fabric in the order given unless otherwise noted. The appliqué patterns are on page 91. Refer to "Kim's Invisible Machine-Appliqué Technique" on page 116 or substitute your own favorite method.

From the tan print, cut:

1 strip, 20½" × 42"; crosscut 1 square, 20½" × 20½". From the remainder of this strip, cut 1 square, 10½" × 10½".

1 strip, 10½" × 42"; crosscut into 3 squares, 10½" × 10½"

7 strips, 5½" × 42"; crosscut into 44 squares, 5½" × 5½"

From the *bias* of the ½ yard of green print, cut:

12 strips, 1¼" × 10"

8 strips, 1¼" × 7"

Reserve the scraps for the appliqués.

From the reserved green print and the 3 coordinating green fat quarters, cut a *combined total* of:

120 large leaves

16 small leaves

16 reversed small leaves

From the dark blue print, cut:

4 birds

From the medium blue print, cut:

4 bird wings

From the brown or black print, cut:

4 vases

From the red print, cut:

8 strips, 3" × 42"; crosscut into 92 squares, 3" × 3"

7 binding strips, 2½" × 42" (see "Completing the Quilt" on page 89)

4 flowers

From the cheddar or gold print, cut:

4 stars

Piecing for One Old Italian Block

The instructions that follow will make one block. Use the pieces cut for one block and repeat as many times as needed to make the required number of blocks. Sew all pieces with right sides together using a ¼" seam allowance unless otherwise noted. Press the seam allowances as indicated by the arrows or as otherwise specified.

1. Select one 4¾" square, one 1½" square from a second print, and four matching 1½" × 4" rectangles from a third print. Cut the 4¾" square into quarters diagonally to yield four triangles.

2. Lay out the pieces cut for one block in three diagonal rows as shown. Join the pieces in each diagonal row; press. Join the rows; press.

Using Directional Prints

Using a directional print or stripe for the triangle portions of the Old Italian block can provide wonderful design opportunities. If you use triangles cut from a single square, they can be positioned so that the print flows in one direction. Using two squares to cut the triangles will enable you to choose the pieces you'd like, positioning them in such a way as to give the illusion that the print radiates out from the block center or wraps around, and you'll have enough triangles to make two blocks. For the featured quilt, both triangle options were incorporated for an interesting variety in the look of the blocks.

 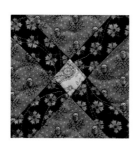

Streamlined Stitching

I found it was helpful to lay out the pieces for each block next to my sewing machine, layering six to eight blocks at a time. Layering the pieces allowed me to audition the placement of any directional prints and keep them positioned in the way I intended while I pinned and joined the units. I simply worked my way through the stack to join the pieces in each diagonal row, and then replaced the pieced units in their original positions alongside the prints they matched, enabling me to keep the layers in the proper order. Easy!

Stitching the Yo-Yos

From the assorted print charm squares, use the Clover small yo-yo maker (and the manufacturer's instructions) with the perle cotton and a size 5 embroidery needle to cut and stitch a total of 156 yo-yos. With careful placement of the yo-yo maker, you can cut two yo-yos from opposite corners of each charm square. Use additional scraps, if needed, to make the required number of yo-yos and achieve a good balance of color.

3. Use a rotary cutter and an acrylic ruler to trim away the corners and square up the block to measure 5½" square, including the seam allowances.

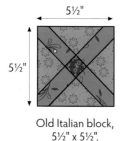

Old Italian block,
5½" x 5½".

4. Repeat steps 1–3 to make a total of 68 Old Italian blocks.

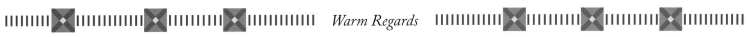

Appliquéing the Center Block

1. With *wrong* sides together, fold each of the green bias strips in half lengthwise and use a scant ¼" seam allowance to stitch along the long raw edges to make tubes. Use the bias bar to press the tubes flat, centering the seam allowances so they'll be hidden from the front. Apply small dots of liquid fabric glue underneath the pressed seam allowance of each stem at approximately ½" intervals, and use a hot, dry iron to heat set the seams from the back of the stem and anchor them in place.

2. Fold the tan 20½" square in half diagonally right sides together, and use a hot, dry iron to lightly press the center crease. Unfold the square and repeat to press a second diagonal crease, and then vertical and horizontal creases.

3. Trace the vine guide (page 90) onto freezer paper and cut it out. Fold the prepared guide in half to find the center; finger-press a crease. Align this crease with a pressed vertical or horizontal crease of the tan square, aligning

the straight edges of the guide with the raw edge of the square; iron the template to the square. Dot the background of the square with liquid fabric glue a few threads out from the curved vine guide.

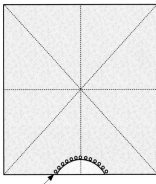

Dot glue around template.

4. Position a 10"-long stem onto the background exactly next to the guide edge, extending the excess length beyond the square edges on each side of the guide. Remove the guide and repeat with the remaining sides of the square. Heat

83

set the stems from the wrong side of the square. Do *not* trim away the excess stem length.

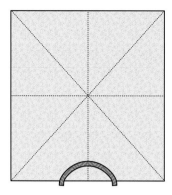

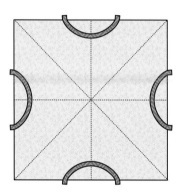

5. Measure 8" from one corner along the diagonal and make a small pencil mark on the crease. On the same corner, measure 1½" from the corner and place a second mark on the crease. Dot the crease between the pencil marks with liquid fabric glue at approximately ½" intervals. Beginning at the 8" mark, center one end of a 10"-long stem over the square crease, running the stem along the length of the crease and extending the excess beyond the corner of the square. Repeat with the remaining block corners. Heat set the stems from the back of the square. Do *not* trim away the excess stem length.

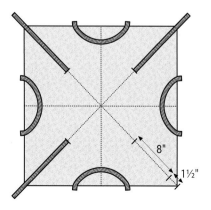

6. On the flat side of a yo-yo, apply seven or eight dots of liquid fabric glue around the perimeter of the circle, approximately ⅛" from the edge; add one additional glue dot in the yo-yo center. Position the yo-yo onto the tip of a diagonal stem so the center of the yo-yo is over the end of the stem. Repeat to add yo-yos to the remaining diagonal stems. Heat set the yo-yos from the back of the tan square, pressing firmly to affix them to the square and slightly flatten the gathered centers.

7. Referring to the diagram below and the pictured quilt, lay out six leaves along one diagonal stem, positioning the outermost leaves approximately ¾" in from the raw square edges; pin in place. Repeat with an adjacent corner of the square. Next, position a bird onto the curved side stem between the prepared corners, positioning the bird so it fits between the leaves of the diagonal stems; pin. Last, lay out two small leaves and two small reversed leaves along the curved stem.

8. Continue working along each side and corner of the square as described in step 6 to lay out the remaining bird and leaf appliqués. When you're pleased with the arrangement, use your favorite appliqué method to stitch all of the pieces in place, leaving the bottom 1½" portion of each diagonal stem unstitched. Appliqué a wing onto each bird. Trim away the excess length of the curved side stems, but do *not* trim any length from the diagonal corner stems.

9. Using the pictured quilt (page 80) and the crease marks as guides, and working on a large flat surface, lay out nine yo-yos above the yo-yo at the tip of a diagonal stem. Repeat with the remaining quadrants of the square. When you're pleased with the arrangement, glue baste, heat set, and stitch the yo-yos as previously instructed.

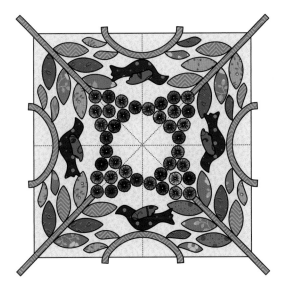

Appliquéing the Vase Blocks

1. Press two diagonal creases, corner to corner, onto each tan 10½" square as described in step 1 of "Appliquéing the Center Block" (page 83).

2. Fold a vase appliqué in half and finger-press a center crease. Position the vase onto one corner of prepared tan square, aligning the creases and placing the bottom vase corners approximately ¾" in from each raw square edge; pin in place.

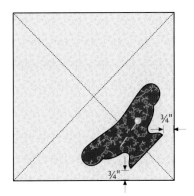

3. Dot the diagonal crease above the vase with liquid fabric glue, stopping 2" from the top corner. Center a 10" stem onto the square crease, tucking the bottom raw edge under the vase approximately ¼", and extending the

stem to the top corner of the square. (The top 2" of the stem is unglued at this time.)

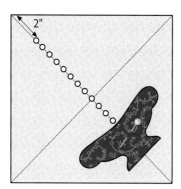

4. Position a red flower approximately 3" above the top of the vase, centering it over the stem; pin. Pin a large leaf to each side of the stem, approximately 1" above the top of the vase. Next, glue baste and position a 7"-long stem onto the tan background at each side of the center stem, tucking the raw edges of the stems under the vase approximately ¼" and flaring them out to rest on the diagonal corner creases.

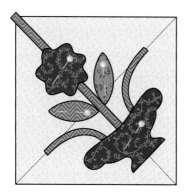

5. Using the pictured quilt as a guide, cluster three yo-yos onto each side corner of the square, trimming away any excess stem length to hide the tips under the middle yo-yos. Position a yo-yo onto each side of the center stem, just above the flower. Glue baste and heat set the yo-yos.

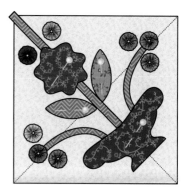

6. Position and pin two small leaves and two small reversed leaves to the side stems of the square. Stitch the appliqués in place, leaving the stem above the flower unstitched and untrimmed. Last, appliqué a star to the center of the red flower.

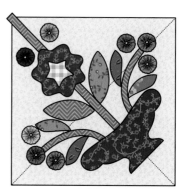

7. Repeat steps 2–6 for a total of four appliquéd vase blocks.

toward the vase block. Repeat to make a total of four corner block units measuring 15½" square, including the seam allowances.

Assembling the Quilt Top

1. Lay out 12 Old Italian blocks in three rows of four blocks each. Join the blocks in each row; press. Join the rows; press. Repeat to make a total of four side block units measuring 15½" × 20½", including the seam allowances.

Make 4 units,
15½" x 20½".

Make 4 corner units,
15½" x 15½".

3. Referring to the quilt assembly diagram on page 89, position a side block unit on the right and left sides of the appliquéd center block, with the seam allowances of the side units directed away from the center block. Pin the unsewn portions of the corner stems away from the block corners. Join the pieces. Press the seam allowances toward the center block.

2. Join two Old Italian blocks; press. Make a second unit of three Old Italian blocks joined end to end; press. Lay out one vase block and the two pieced block units as shown. Join the double block unit to the vase block; press. Join the remaining block unit to the adjacent side of the vase block. Press the seam allowances

4. Pin the unsewn portions of the vase block stems away from the corners. Using the pictured quilt (page 80) as a guide, join a corner block unit to each short side of a side block unit. Press the seam allowances toward the corner block units. Repeat to make two units. Join these units to the top and bottom of the step 3 unit. Press the seam allowances toward the center block.

5. Unpin all of the stems at the block corners. Position a yo-yo onto the stem of each vase block, slightly beyond the two yo-yos resting above the flowers. Trim the center block stems and the vase block stems so the raw ends rest together under the newly added yo-yos. Stitch the unsewn portion of the stems, and then the yo-yos, ensuring the raw stem ends are hidden.

Making and Adding the Border

1. Using a pencil and an acrylic ruler, draw a diagonal sewing line from corner to corner on the wrong side of each red 3" square.

2. Layer a prepared red square onto one corner of a tan 5½" square. Stitch the pair together along the drawn line. Fold the resulting inner triangle open, aligning the raw edges with the corner of the tan square; press. Trim away the excess layers beneath the top triangle, leaving a ¼" seam allowance. In the same manner, layer, stitch, press, and trim a second red square to the adjacent corner to form a mirror-image point. Repeat to make a total of 44 border blocks measuring 5½" square, including the seam allowances.

Make 44.

3. Select four pieced border blocks from step 2. Layer, stitch, press, and trim one additional red 3" square to each block to make four border corner blocks measuring 5½" square, including the seam allowances.

Make 4.

4. Fold each step 2 border block in half, with the two red triangles together, and lightly press a center crease.

5. Using the pictured quilt as a guide, position and baste a large leaf on each side of the center crease of a border block. Glue baste, position, and heat set a yo-yo above the two leaves, centering it onto the background crease. Repeat with the remaining step 2 blocks. Appliqué the blocks.

6. Position, glue baste, and stitch two large leaves and one yo-yo onto each step 3 border corner block.

7. Referring to the quilt assembly diagram on page 89, join 10 appliquéd border blocks end to end. Press the seam allowances open. Repeat to make a total of four pieced border strips measuring 5½" × 50½", including the seam allowances.

8. Position, glue baste, and heat set a yo-yo onto each seam joining the appliquéd border blocks, placing the yo-yos a scant ½" down from the tan raw edge. Repeat with the remaining three pieced border strips.

9. Join a step 8 border strip to the right and left sides of the quilt top. Press.

10. Join an appliquéd corner block to each end of the remaining border strips. Press. Join these strips to the remaining sides of the quilt top. Press.

Completing the Quilt

Layer and baste the quilt top, batting, and backing. Quilt the layers. The featured quilt was machine quilted with a feathered wreath and crosshatch design in the middle of the center block. A diagonal crosshatch was stitched between the curved side stems and block edges, and a small-scale pebbling design was stitched onto the open background areas. The backgrounds of the vase blocks were echo quilted, straight lines were stitched onto the vases using the striped print as a guide, and all of the appliqués were outlined to emphasize their shapes. The Old Italian blocks were quilted with squared feathered wreaths radiating out from the center squares. Small pebbling was stitched onto the tan background portion of the border, and concentric straight lines were stitched onto the red triangle patchwork. Referring to "Kim's Chubby Binding" on page 127, or substituting your favorite method, use the red binding strips to bind the quilt.

Quilt assembly

Pincushions from Repurposed Orphan Blocks

When I make scrappy quilts, I like to stitch a handful of extra blocks for added choices as the design is laid out. I found that my leftover "orphan" Old Italian blocks from this project could be repurposed beautifully to make sweet little pincushions. To do this, I layered a finished block with a coordinating print 5½" square, right sides together, and joined the pieces, leaving a 2" opening on one side for turning.

Next, to box the corners, I pulled the front and back pieces apart at one corner, laid the unit flat on my cutting mat with the corner pointing upward and the seam centered and running vertically, and used a pencil and acrylic ruler to draw a horizontal line across the corner (through the seam) ½" down from the stitched point. After pinning, I repeated with the remaining corners, and then stitched each corner on the drawn line (beginning and ending with a few backstitches), before trimming away the corners to leave ¼" seam allowances.

To complete the pincushion, I then turned the unit right side out, filled it with crushed walnut shells (which was easy to do using a quart-size ziplock bag and snipping one corner for pouring), and hand stitched the opening. These are super fast to stitch, super cute, and make great gifts for quilting friends. ~ Kim

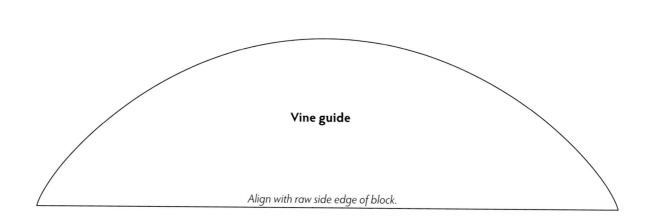

Vine guide

Align with raw side edge of block.

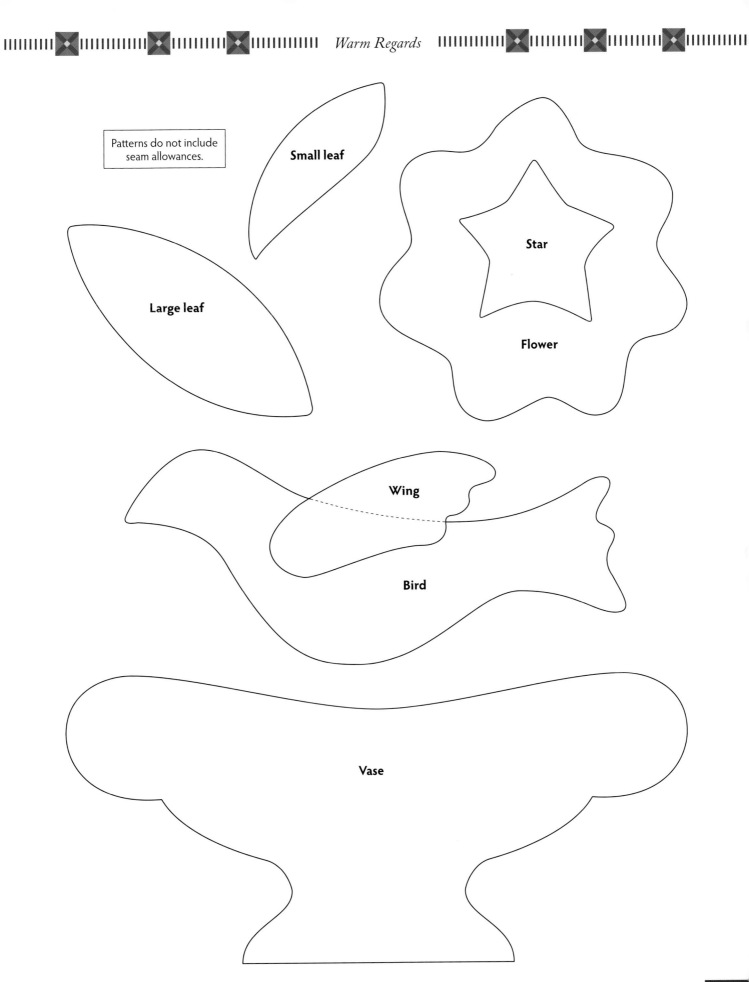

Patterns do not include seam allowances.

Small leaf

Star

Large leaf

Flower

Wing

Bird

Vase

Each Old Italian block in this quilt uses two fabrics: one for the X and one for the background. To really make each block stand on its own, I separated the blocks from one another with sashing. (The sashing also makes it easier to match and join the blocks, so it's doing double duty as a design element and a facilitator!) Notice the border. I chose a directional print, but rather than orienting the print in the same direction on all four sides of the quilt, I cut lengthwise strips and positioned them so that the flowers run continuously around the quilt, with the border print facing in opposite directions on opposite sides on the quilt. ~ Jo

Swap Talk

This little quilt is made using 36 blocks, so it's perfect for a small group exchange. My group had six members, so we each made six sets of blocks containing six blocks each. That means we each made a total of 36 blocks, but because we swapped with friends, we ended up with a wider variety of fabrics in our finished quilts than if we had made them all ourselves. Just be sure to specify the colors or values you'd like so your finished quilt will be one that you love!

Materials

Yardage is based on 42" of usable fabric width after prewashing and removing selvages. Fat eighths are 9" × 21".

Approximately ⅔ yard *total* of assorted light tan, cream, and blue prints for block crosses

Approximately 1 yard *total* of assorted medium to dark brown and teal prints for block backgrounds

⅝ yard of light tan print for sashing

1 fat eighth of medium brown print for cornerstones

1¼ yards of blue-and-brown floral for border

¼ yard of tan print for single-fold binding

2½ yards of fabric for backing

45" × 45" square of batting

Finished quilt size:
38⅝" × 38⅝"

Finished exchange block size: 4" × 4"

Designed by Jo Morton. Pieced by Sheri Dowding, Mary Fornoff, Cindy Hansen, and Phyllis Masters. Quilted by Maggi Honeyman.

Cutting

You'll need 36 Old Italian blocks to complete the featured quilt. For ease in piecing the blocks, keep the pieces for each block together as you cut them.

CUTTING FOR
1 OLD ITALIAN BLOCK

From the *lengthwise grain* of 1 light print, cut:*
4 rectangles, 1⅜" × 3¼"

From 1 medium or dark print, cut:
1 square, 1⅜" × 1⅜"
1 square, 4⅛" × 4⅛"; cut in half diagonally *twice* to yield 4 triangles**

*Jo recommends cutting these pieces on the lengthwise grain of the fabric (parallel to the selvage), because it has the least amount of stretch and will give you nice, straight edges.

**If you're using a stripe or directional print, cut 2 squares, 3" × 3", and cut each square in half diagonally. Careful cutting of strips will let you add movement to your blocks.

ADDITIONAL CUTTING

Cut all pieces across the width of the fabric in the order given unless otherwise noted.

From the *lengthwise grain* of the light tan print, cut:*
84 rectangles, 1⅜" × 4½"

From the medium brown print, cut:
49 squares, 1⅜" × 1⅜"

From the *lengthwise grain* of the blue-and-brown floral, cut:*
2 strips, 4½" × 30⅝"
2 strips, 4½" × 38⅝"

From the tan print, cut:
5 single-fold binding strips, 1⅛" × 42" (see "Completing the Quilt" on page 97)

*Jo recommends cutting these pieces on the lengthwise grain of the fabric (parallel to the selvage), because it has the least amount of stretch and will give you nice, straight edges.

Piecing for One Old Italian Block

The instructions that follow will make one block. Use the pieces cut for one block and repeat as many times as needed to make the required number of blocks. Sew all pieces with right sides together using a scant ¼" seam allowance unless otherwise noted. Press the seam allowances as indicated by the arrows or as otherwise specified.

1. Arrange the pieces cut for one block in three diagonal rows as shown. Sew the pieces in each row together; press.

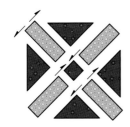

2. Pin and then sew the rows together, matching the seam intersections. Refer to "Jo's Clipping Trick" (page 114) to clip the seam intersections. Press the clipped intersections open and the seam allowances toward the dark print.

3. With the X centered, square up the block to measure 4½" × 4½", including the seam allowances.

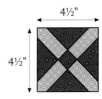

4. Repeat steps 1–3 to make 36 Old Italian blocks.

toward the sashing rectangles. The quilt center should measure 30⅝" square, including the seam allowances.

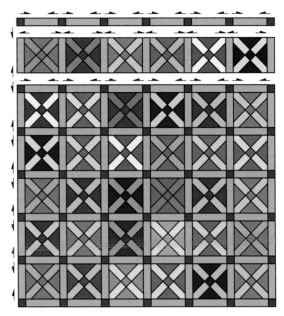

Quilt assembly

Assembling the Quilt Top

1. Lay out six blocks and seven light tan 1⅜" × 4½" sashing rectangles in alternating positions. Join the pieces; press. Repeat to make a total of six block rows measuring 4½" × 30⅝", including the seam allowances.

Make 6 rows,
4½" x 30⅝".

2. Lay out six light tan 1⅜" × 4½" sashing rectangles and seven medium brown 1⅜" sashing squares in alternating positions. Join the pieces; press. Repeat to make a total of seven sashing rows measuring 1⅜" × 30⅝", including the seam allowances.

Make 7 rows,
1⅜" x 30⅝".

3. Referring to the quilt assembly diagram above right, lay out the block and sashing rows in alternating positions. Join the rows. Clip the seam intersections. Press the clipped intersections open and the seam allowances

Sewing in Quadrants

I find it much easier to sew smaller sections together, rather than working in long rows. For this quilt, lay out the pieces on your design wall. When you're satisfied with the placement of the blocks, "divide" the quilt in half at the horizontal center sashing row, giving the pieces of that sashing row to either the top or bottom half. Then divide each half along the vertical center sashing row, giving the pieces of that sashing row to either the right or left side. Now, sew the pieces in each block row and each sashing row of each quadrant together, and then join the rows to complete each quadrant. Join the quadrants to make two halves, and then join the halves. Sewing one long seam is much easier than 13! ~ Jo

4. With the print oriented upward (if using a directional motif as in the quilt shown), join a floral 4½" × 30⅝" border strip to the left edge of the quilt top; press. Join another border strip to the right edge, positioning the print (if directional) so it is directed downward. Press the seam allowances toward the border. Join the floral 4½" × 38⅝" border strips to the top and bottom edges of the quilt top, with the print (if directional) facing toward the right on the top strip and toward the left on the

bottom strip. This way the print direction runs clockwise around the perimeter of the quilt. Press the seam allowances toward the border.

Completing the Quilt

Layer and baste the quilt top, batting, and backing. Quilt the layers. The featured quilt was quilted by machine. Referring to "Jo's Single-Fold Binding" (page 126), or substituting your favorite method, join the tan print strips into one length and use it to bind the quilt.

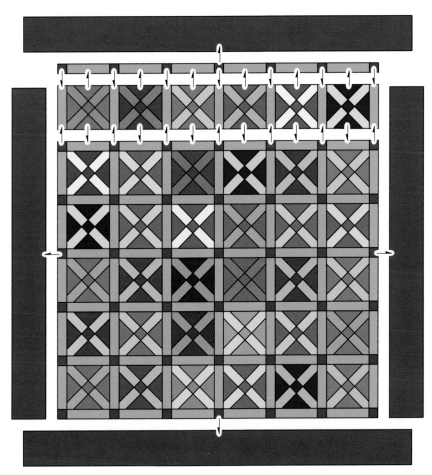

Adding borders

Chocolate Factory is a row quilt (my first one ever!) that includes each of the block designs I used in this book. I chose a palette of mellow browns and creams for a two-color quilt. It may be just two colors, but it uses many different prints. You might want to make it as a block swap where each quilter in the group is responsible for one of the rows, or mix it up with each participant making one or more of the different blocks. Or, simply make it on your own with your scrap basket at the ready! ~ Jo

Materials

Yardage is based on 42" of usable fabric width after prewashing and removing selvages. Fat quarters are 18" × 21".

Approximately ¾ yard *total* of assorted tan and cream shirting prints for blocks

Approximately ⅝ yard *total* of assorted dark brown prints for blocks

Approximately ½ yard *total* of assorted medium brown prints for blocks

6 fat quarters of assorted brown prints for row setting triangles

⅛ yard *each* of 5 assorted brown prints for sashing strips

1¼ yards of medium brown print for border

¼ yard of dark brown print for single-fold binding

2⅛ yards of fabric for backing

37" × 47" piece of batting

Cutting

The instructions that follow are for cutting all of the pieces needed to make the quilt top. For ease in piecing the blocks, keep the pieces for each block or set of blocks grouped together as you cut them.

EVENING STAR BLOCKS

Repeat 5 times, using a different set of prints for each block.

From 1 medium brown print scrap, cut:
4 squares, 1⅞" × 1⅞"

From 1 dark brown print, cut:
1 square, 3¼" × 3¼"
4 squares, 1½" × 1½"

From a second dark brown print, cut:
1 square, 2½" × 2½"

Continued on page 100

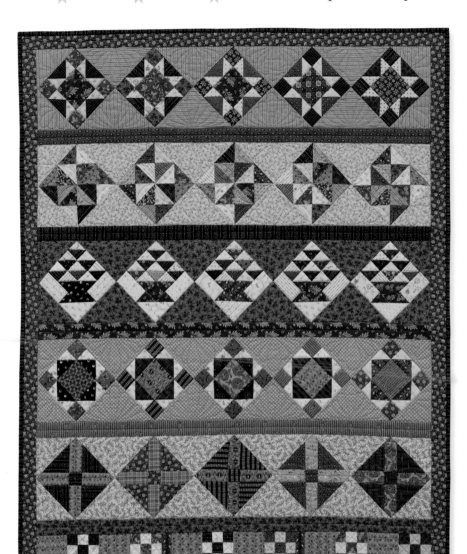

Finished quilt size: 30¾" × 40¼"

Designed by Jo Morton. Pieced by Sheri Dowding, Mary Fornoff, Cindy Hansen, and Phyllis Masters. Machine quilted by Maggi Honeyman.

Continued from page 98

YANKEE PUZZLE BLOCKS

From the assorted tan and cream shirting prints, cut a *total* of:
10 squares, 3¼" × 3¼"

From the assorted medium and dark brown prints, cut a *total* of:
10 squares, 3¼" × 3¼"

BASKET BLOCKS

From the assorted tan and cream shirting prints, cut a *total* of:
15 squares, 2" × 2"
5 squares, 1⅞" × 1⅞"; cut each square in half diagonally *once* to yield 2 small triangles (combined total of 10)

From the assorted medium and dark brown prints, cut a *total* of:
15 squares, 2" × 2"

From the assorted cream shirting prints, cut a *total* of:

5 squares, 2⅞" × 2⅞"; cut each square in half diagonally *once* to yield 2 large triangles (combined total of 10; you'll use 1 triangle from each print and have 5 left over)

From *each* of 5 cream shirting prints, cut:

2 rectangles, 1½" × 2½" (combined total of 10)

From *each* of 5 dark brown prints, cut:

1 square, 2⅞" × 2⅞"; cut in half diagonally *once* to yield 2 large triangles (combined total of 10; you'll use 1 triangle from each print and have 5 left over)
1 square, 1⅞" × 1⅞"; cut in half diagonally *once* to yield 2 small triangles (combined total of 10)

KING'S CROWN BLOCKS

Repeat 5 times, using a different set of prints for each block.

From 1 cream shirting print, cut:

4 squares, 1⅞" × 1⅞"

From 1 dark brown print, cut:

1 square, 3¼" × 3¼"

From 1 medium brown print or a different dark brown print, cut:

4 squares, 1½" × 1½"

From a second medium brown print, cut:

1 square, 2½" × 2½"

OLD ITALIAN BLOCKS

Repeat 5 times, using a different set of prints for each block.

From the *lengthwise grain* of 1 cream shirting print, cut:*

4 rectangles, 1⅜" × 3¼"

From 1 medium or dark brown print, cut:

1 square, 1⅜" × 1⅜"
1 square, 4⅛" × 4⅛"; cut in half diagonally *twice* to yield 4 triangles**

NINE PATCH BLOCKS

Repeat 12 times, using a different set of prints for each block.

From 1 medium or dark brown print, cut:

5 squares, 1¼" × 1¼"

From 1 cream shirting print, cut:

4 squares, 1¼" × 1¼"

ADDITIONAL CUTTING

Cut all pieces across the width of the fabric in the order given unless otherwise noted.

From *each* of 5 brown fat quarters for setting triangles, cut:

2 squares, 7¼" × 7¼"; cut each square in half diagonally *twice* to yield 4 side setting triangles (combined total of 8)
2 squares, 4" × 4"; cut each square in half diagonally *once* to yield 2 corner setting triangles (combined total of 4)

From the remaining brown fat quarter, cut:

12 squares, 2¾" × 2¾"

From 1 dark brown print, cut:

2 rectangles, 1⅛" × 5"

From *each* of the 5 brown prints for sashing strips, cut:

1 strip, 1½" × 28¾" (combined total of 5)

From the *lengthwise grain* of the medium brown print for border, cut:*

2 strips, 1½" × 38¼"
2 strips, 1½" × 30¾"

From the dark brown print for binding, cut:

4 single-fold binding strips, 1⅛" × 42" (see "Completing the Quilt" on page 103)

*Jo recommends cutting these pieces on the lengthwise grain of the fabric (parallel to the selvage), because it has the least amount of stretch and will give you nice, straight edges.

**If you're using a stripe or directional print, cut 2 squares, 3" × 3", and cut each square in half diagonally. Careful cutting of stripes will let you add movement to your blocks.

Piecing the Block Rows

Sew all pieces with right sides together using a scant ¼" seam allowance unless otherwise noted. Press the seam allowances as indicated by the arrows or as otherwise specified.

1. Using the pieces cut for the Evening Star blocks, refer to "Piecing for One Evening Star Block" (page 9) to make five blocks.

2. Choose one set of brown setting triangles. Lay out the blocks and setting triangles in five diagonal rows as shown. Join the pieces in each row; press. Join the rows; press. Add the remaining corner triangles last; press.

3. Square up the row to measure 6⅛" × 28¾", including the seam allowances.

4. Using the pieces cut for the Yankee Puzzle blocks, refer to "Piecing for One Yankee Puzzle Block" (page 59) to make five blocks. Repeat steps 2 and 3 above to make the Yankee Puzzle row.

5. Using the pieces cut for the Basket blocks, refer to step 1 of "Piecing for One Basket Block" (page 67) to make 30 half-square-triangle units from the medium or dark brown 2" squares and light brown or cream 2" squares.

6. Referring to steps 2–6 of "Piecing for One Basket Block" and using six half-square-triangle units, two light brown or cream small triangles, one dark brown large triangle, two matching dark brown small triangles, two matching cream rectangles, and one cream large triangle for each block, make a total of five Basket blocks.

7. Repeat steps 2 and 3 above to make the Basket block row.

8. Using the pieces cut for the King's Crown blocks, refer to "Piecing for One King's Crown Block" (page 33) to make five blocks. Repeat steps 2 and 3 at left to make the King's Crown row.

9. Using the pieces cut for the Old Italian blocks, refer to "Piecing for One Old Italian Block" (page 95) to make five blocks. Repeat steps 2 and 3 at left to make the Old Italian row.

10. Using the pieces cut for the Nine Patch blocks, lay out five brown squares and four cream squares in three horizontal rows, alternating the cream and brown squares in each row and from row to row. Join the squares in each row; press the seam allowances toward the brown squares. Pin and sew the rows together, matching the seam intersections. Refer to "Jo's Clipping Trick" (page 114) to clip the seam intersections. Press the clipped intersections open and the seam allowances toward the brown squares. The block should measure 2¾" square, including the seam allowances. Repeat to make a total of 12 blocks.

11. Lay out two Nine Patch blocks and two brown 2¾" squares in two horizontal rows as shown. Sew the pieces in each row together. Press the seam allowances toward the brown squares. Pin and then sew the rows together, matching the seam intersections. Using "Jo's Clipping Trick," clip the seam intersections. Press the clipped intersections open and the seam allowances toward the brown print. Make six four-patch units. Square up each unit to 5" square, including the seam allowances.

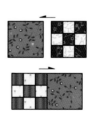

Make 6 blocks,
5" x 5".

12. Sew the four-patch units together side by side in pairs. Clip the seam intersection. Press the clipped intersections open and the seam allowances toward the brown squares. Repeat to make a total of three units.

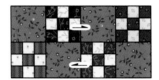

Make 3 units,
5" x 9½".

13. Referring to the pictured quilt on page 100, lay out the blocks and the two dark brown 1⅛" × 5" rectangles in one horizontal row. Join the pieces. Press the seam allowances toward the dark brown rectangles. Square up the row to measure 5" × 28¾", including the seam allowances.

Assembling the Quilt Top

1. Referring to the pictured quilt, lay out the pieced rows and assorted brown 1½" × 28¾" sashing strips in alternating positions. Pin and then sew the rows and sashing strips together. Press the seam allowances toward the sashing strips. The pieced quilt top should measure 28¾" × 38¼", including the seam allowances.

2. Sew the medium brown 1½" × 38¼" border strips to the right and left sides of the quilt top. Press the seam allowances toward the border. Add the medium brown 1½" × 30¾" strips to the top and bottom of the quilt top. Press the seam allowances toward the border.

Completing the Quilt

Layer and baste the quilt top, batting, and backing. Quilt the layers. The featured quilt was quilted by machine. Referring to "Jo's Single-Fold Binding" (page 126), or substituting your favorite method, join the dark brown strips into one length and use it to bind the quilt.

This spectacular sampler quilt showcases a variety of rich red prints, with a sprinkling of this book's exchange block designs set into Star block centers for extra sparkle. I stitched the yo-yos for my project as I waited in Labor and Delivery for the arrival of my beautiful grandbaby Ruby, the inspiration for this quilt. ~ Kim

Materials

Yardage is based on 42" of usable fabric width after prewashing and removing selvages. Fat quarters are 18" × 21", fat eighths are 9" × 21", chubby sixteenths are 9" × 10½", and charm squares are 5" × 5". For greater ease in selecting fabrics for this sampler-style quilt, yardage for the various red prints used for the quilt center is provided on a block-by-block basis, followed by additional fabric requirements and items needed to complete the quilt. Reserve the scraps from the various red prints to make the appliqués and yo-yos.

NINE PATCH STAR BLOCKS

1 chubby sixteenth of red print A for Nine Patch blocks

1 chubby sixteenth of medium red check for framing corner squares

1 fat quarter of coordinating red print B for star points

YANKEE PUZZLE STAR BLOCKS

1 fat quarter of dark red print E for star points

1 fat eighth of red print F for Yankee Puzzle blocks

KING'S CROWN STAR BLOCKS

1 fat eighth of dark red print C for King's Crown blocks

½ yard of medium red check for King's Crown blocks and middle-border vines

1 fat quarter of red print D for star points

SMALL MOSAIC STAR BLOCKS

1 fat eighth of red print G for blocks

CAKE STAND BLOCKS

1 fat eighth of red print H for cake-stand bases

4 chubby sixteenths of assorted coordinating red prints I–L for cake-stand handles, appliqués, and yo-yos

Continued on page 106

Finished quilt size:
62½" × 62½"

Designed by Kim Diehl. Pieced by Jennifer Martinez and Kim Diehl. Machine appliquéd by Kim Diehl. Machine quilted by Leisa Wiggley.

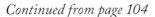

Continued from page 104

ADDITIONAL FABRIC AND SUPPLIES

2¼ yards of light cream print for quilt center patchwork and inner and middle borders

1 yard of red stripe for inner and middle borders, appliqués, yo-yos, and binding

1⅔ yards of medium cream print for middle and outer borders

1 fat quarter of dark red print M for Large Mosaic Star blocks, appliqués, and yo-yos

1 yard of dark red print N for Old Italian blocks and appliqués

1 fat quarter of red print O for Old Italian block centers, appliqués, and yo-yos

Scraps of additional assorted red prints for appliqués and yo-yos (optional)

4 yards of fabric for backing

71" × 71" square of batting

Bias bar to make ⅜" stems

Liquid glue for fabric, water-soluble and acid-free (Kim likes the results achieved with Quilter's Choice Basting Glue by Beacon Adhesives)

Clover small yo-yo maker

#12 or #8 perle cotton for stitching yo-yos (Kim used Valdani's variegated #12 perle cotton in color H212 Faded Brown)

Size 5 embroidery needle

Supplies for your favorite appliqué method

Cutting

The instructions that follow are for cutting all of the pieces needed to make the quilt top. Cut all pieces across the width of the fabric in the order given unless otherwise noted. For ease in piecing the blocks, keep the pieces for each block grouped together as you cut them. Reserve the scraps from all red prints for later use in stitching the appliqués and yo-yos, as instructed in "Appliquéing and Adding the Middle Border" (page 111).

NINE PATCH STAR BLOCKS

From red print A, cut:
20 squares, 1½" × 1½"

From the medium red check, cut:
16 squares, 1" × 1"

From red print B, cut:
32 squares, 2½" × 2½"

From the light cream print, cut:
1 strip, 1½" × 42"; crosscut into 16 squares, 1½" × 1½"
2 strips, 1" × 42"; crosscut into 16 rectangles, 1" × 3½"
3 strips, 2½" × 42"; crosscut into:
    16 rectangles, 2½" × 4½"
    16 squares, 2½" × 2½"

YANKEE PUZZLE STAR BLOCKS
From dark red print E, cut:
32 squares, 2½" × 2½"

From red print F, cut:
8 squares, 3¼" × 3¼"; cut each square in half diagonally *once* to yield a total of 16 triangles

From the light cream print, cut:
1 strip, 3¼" × 42"; crosscut into 8 squares, 3¼" × 3¼". Cut each square in half diagonally *once* to yield a total of 16 triangles.
3 strips, 2½" × 42"; crosscut into:
    16 rectangles, 2½" × 4½"
    16 squares, 2½" × 2½"

KING'S CROWN STAR BLOCKS

From red print C, cut:
5 squares, 2½" × 2½"
20 squares, 1½" × 1½"

From the medium red check, cut:
2 strips, 1½" × 42"; crosscut into 20 rectangles, 1½" × 2½"
Reserve the remainder of the fabric.

From red print D, cut:
40 squares, 2½" × 2½"

From the light cream print, cut:
2 strips, 1½" × 42"; crosscut into 40 squares, 1½" × 1½"
4 strips, 2½" × 42"; crosscut into:
    20 rectangles, 2½" × 4½"
    20 squares, 2½" × 2½"

SMALL MOSAIC STAR BLOCKS

From red print G, cut:
48 squares, 1½" × 1½"

From the light cream print, cut:
3 strips, 2½" × 42"; crosscut into:
    8 rectangles, 2½" × 8½"
    8 rectangles, 2½" × 4½"
    4 squares, 2½" × 2½"
2 strips, 1½" × 42"; crosscut into:
    16 rectangles, 1½" × 2½"
    16 squares, 1½" × 1½"

CAKE STAND BLOCKS

From red print H, cut:
4 squares, 2⅞" × 2⅞"; cut each square in half diagonally *once* to yield a total of 8 triangles
16 squares, 1½" × 1½"

From *each* of red prints I–L, cut:
4 squares, 1⅞" × 1⅞" (combined total of 16); cut each square in half diagonally *once* to yield 2 triangles (combined total of 32)

Continued on page 108

Continued from page 107

From the light cream print, cut:

1 strip, 2⅞" × 42"; crosscut into 4 squares,
2⅞" × 2⅞". Cut each square in half diagonally
once to yield 2 triangles (combined total of 8).
1 strip, 1⅞" × 42"; crosscut into 16 squares,
1⅞" × 1⅞". Cut each square in half diagonally
once to yield 2 triangles (combined total of 32).
2 strips, 1½" × 42"; crosscut into:
16 rectangles, 1½" × 2½"
8 squares, 1½" × 1½"
6 strips, 2½" × 42"; crosscut into:
16 rectangles, 2½" × 8½"
16 rectangles, 2½" × 4½"
8 squares, 2½" × 2½"
Reserve the remainder of the fabric for the
following cutting instructions.

ADDITIONAL CUTTING

From the red stripe, cut:

6 strips, 1½" × 42"; crosscut into:
4 strips, 1½" × 40½"
8 rectangles, 1½" × 5½"
7 binding strips, 2½" × 42" (see "Completing the
Quilt" on page 112)
Reserve the remainder of the fabric for the
appliqués and yo-yos.

From the reserved remainder of the light cream print, cut:

1 strip, 1¾" × 42"; crosscut into 16 squares,
1¾" × 1¾"
4 squares, 1½" × 1½"

From the medium cream print, cut:

4 strips, 5½" × 42"; crosscut into 4 strips,
5½" × 40½"
2 strips, 1¾" × 42"; crosscut into:
16 rectangles, 1¾" × 3"
16 squares, 1¾" × 1¾"
18 strips, 1½" × 42"; crosscut into:
8 rectangles, 1½" × 5½"
160 rectangles, 1½" × 4"

From dark red print M, cut:

4 squares, 3" × 3"
32 squares, 1¾" × 1¾"

From the *bias* of the reserved medium red check, cut:

12 strips, 1¼" × 8"
8 strips, 1¼" × 16"

From dark red print N, cut:

5 strips, 4¾" × 42"; crosscut into 40 squares,
4¾" × 4¾". Cut each square in half diagonally
twice to yield 4 triangles (combined total of 160).
Reserve the remainder of the fabric for the
appliqués.

From red print O, cut:

40 squares, 1½" × 1½"
4 squares, 5½" × 5½"
Reserve the remainder of the fabric for
the appliqués and yo-yos.

Piecing the Sampler Star Blocks

*Sew all pieces with right sides together using a ¼"
seam allowance unless otherwise noted. Press the
seam allowances as indicated by the arrows or as
otherwise specified.*

1. Select the pieces cut for the Nine Patch Star
blocks. Using the red print A and light cream
1½" squares, follow the instructions
in "Piecing for Two Nine Patch Blocks"
(page 45) to make four blocks with dark
corners measuring 3½" square, including the
seam allowances.

2. Join light cream 1" × 3½" rectangles to the
right and left sides of each Nine Patch block.
Join a medium red check 1" square to each
end of the remaining light cream 1" × 3½"
rectangles. Join these rectangles to the
remaining sides of each Nine Patch block. The
four framed Nine Patch blocks should now
measure 4½" square, including the
seam allowances.

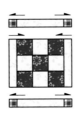

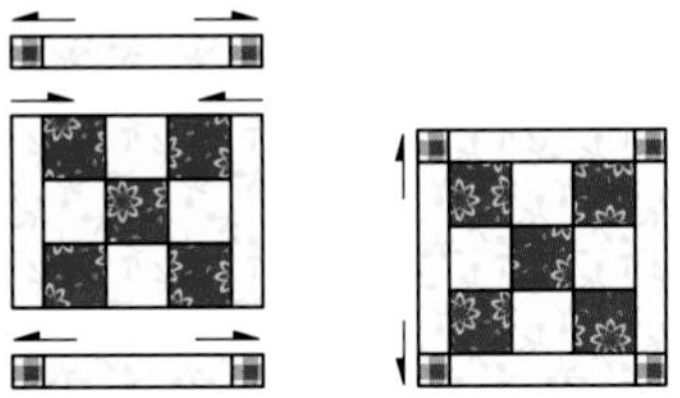

Make 4 blocks,
4½" x 4½".

3. Use a pencil and an acrylic ruler to draw a diagonal sewing line from corner to corner on the wrong side of each red print B 2½" square. Position a prepared square onto one end of a light cream 2½" × 4½" rectangle. Stitch the pair together along the drawn line. Fold the resulting inner triangle open, aligning the corner with the corner of the light cream rectangle; press. Trim away the layers beneath the top triangle, leaving a ¼" seam allowance. In the same manner, add a mirror-image point to the opposite end of the light cream rectangle. Repeat to make a total of 16 flying-geese star-point units.

4. Join flying-geese star-point units to the right and left sides of a framed Nine Patch block. Join light cream 2½" squares to the ends of the two remaining flying-geese units. Join these units to the remaining sides of the Nine Patch blocks. Repeat to make a total of four Nine Patch Star Blocks measuring 8½" square, including the seam allowances.

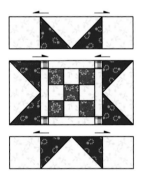 

Make 4 blocks,
8½" x 8½".

5. Using the pieces cut for the Yankee Puzzle Star blocks, follow the instructions in "Piecing for One Yankee Puzzle Block" (page 52) to make four blocks measuring 4½" square, including the seam allowances. Repeat steps 3 and 4 to make the star-point units and add

them to each Yankee Puzzle block. The four blocks should measure 8½" square, including the seam allowances.

Make 4 blocks,
8½" x 8½".

6. Using the pieces cut for the King's Crown Star blocks, follow the instructions in "Piecing for One King's Crown Block" (page 27) to make five blocks measuring 4½" square, including the seam allowances. Repeat steps 3 and 4 to make 20 star-point units and add four of them to each King's Crown block. The five blocks should measure 8½" square, including the seam allowances.

Make 5 blocks,
8½" x 8½".

Piecing the Small Mosaic Star Blocks

1. Using the pieces cut for the Small Mosaic Star blocks, follow the instructions provided in "Piecing for One Mosaic Star Block" (page 15) to make four blocks measuring 4½" square, including the seam allowances.

2. Join a light cream 2½" × 4½" rectangle to the right and left sides of each pieced Mosaic Star block. Press the seam allowances toward the cream rectangles. Join a light cream 2½" × 8½" rectangle to the top and bottom of each Mosaic Star block. Press the seam allowances toward the rectangles. The blocks should measure 8½" square, including the seam allowances.

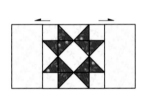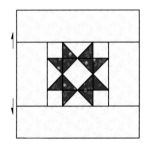

Make 4 blocks,
8½" x 8½".

Piecing the Small Cake Stand Blocks

1. Using the pieces cut for the Cake Stand blocks, follow the instructions in "Piecing for One Cake Stand Block" (page 73) to make eight blocks measuring 4½" square, including the seam allowances.

2. Join a light cream 2½" × 4½" rectangle to the right and left sides of four Cake Stand blocks; press. Join a light cream 2½" × 8½" rectangle to the top and bottom of each block; press. Repeat to make four Small Cake Stand blocks

and four reversed blocks measuring 8½" square, including the seam allowances.

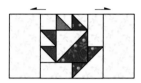

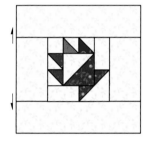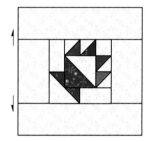

Make 4 of each block,
8½" x 8½".

Assembling the Quilt Top

Referring to the quilt assembly diagram below, lay out the blocks in five horizontal rows. Join the blocks in each row. Press. Join the rows. Press. The pieced quilt center should measure 40½" square, including the seam allowances.

Quilt assembly

ADDING THE INNER BORDER

Join red stripe 1½" × 40½" inner-border strips to the right and left sides of the quilt center. Press the seam allowances toward the border. Join a light cream 1½" square to each end of the remaining red stripe 1½" × 40½" inner-border strips. Press the seam allowances toward the border. Join these pieced strips to the top and bottom of the quilt center. Press the seam allowances toward the borders. The pieced quilt top should measure 42½" square, including the seam allowances.

APPLIQUÉING AND ADDING THE MIDDLE BORDER

The leaf pattern is provided on page 112. Refer to "Kim's Invisible Machine–Appliqué Technique" on page 116 or use your favorite method.

1. Using the Clover small yo-yo maker, the size 5 embroidery needle and perle cotton, and the remaining red prints and scraps, follow the manufacturer's instructions to make 80 yo-yos.

2. From the reserved remainder of the red prints and optional scraps, use your favorite appliqué method to cut and prepare 124 leaves.

3. Fold each of the red check bias strips in half lengthwise with wrong sides together. Use a scant ¼" seam allowance to stitch along the long raw edges to make tubes. Use the bias bar to press the tubes flat, centering the seam allowances so they'll be hidden from the front. Apply small dots of liquid fabric glue underneath the pressed seam allowance of each stem at approximately ½" intervals, and use a hot, dry iron to heat set the seams from the back of the stem and anchor them in place.

4. Dot the seam allowances of three prepared 8" stems and two prepared 16" stems with liquid fabric glue at approximately ½" intervals. Using the pictured quilt (page 106) as a guide, lay out the stems onto a medium cream 5½" × 40½" border strip, aligning the raw ends with the raw border strip edges. From the strip wrong side, use a hot, dry iron to heat set the stems and anchor them in place.

5. Using the pictured quilt as a guide, lay out 31 leaves and 19 yo-yos; pin or baste in place. Use your favorite appliqué method to stitch the leaves and yo-yos.

6. Repeat steps 4 and 5 to make four appliquéd border strips. Appliqué one of the remaining four yo-yos to the center of each Small Mosaic Star block.

7. Referring to "Piecing for One Mosaic Star Block," use the light cream 1¾" squares and the dark red M 3" squares to make four block center square-in-a-square units. Make 16 star-point units, using the medium cream 1¾" × 3" rectangles and the dark red M 1¾" squares. Using one block center unit, four star-point units, and four medium cream 1¾" squares for each block, make four pieced Large Mosaic Star blocks measuring 5½" square, including the seam allowances.

Make 4 blocks,
5½" x 5½".

8. Join a red stripe 1½" × 5½" rectangle to each end of the four appliquéd border strips. Press the seam allowances toward the red rectangles. Join the pieced and appliquéd strips to the right and left sides of the quilt top. Press the seam allowances toward the inner border. Add a Large Mosaic Star block

to each end of the remaining appliquéd border strips. Press the seam allowances away from the blocks. Join these pieced strips to the top and bottom of the quilt top. Press the seam allowances toward the inner border. The pieced quilt top should measure 52½" square, including the seam allowances.

ADDING THE OUTER BORDER

1. Refer to "Piecing for One Old Italian Block" (page 81) to make 40 blocks, using the dark red print N triangles, the medium cream 1½" × 4" rectangles, and the red print O 1½" squares. Each block should measure 5½" square, including the seam allowances.

Make 40 blocks,
5½" x 5½".

2. Join 10 Old Italian blocks end to end. Press the seam allowances open. Join a medium cream 1½" × 5½" rectangle to each end of the pieced strip. Press the seam allowances toward the rectangles. Repeat for a total of four outer-border strips measuring 5½" × 52½", including the seam allowances.

3. Join an outer-border strip to the right and left sides of the quilt top. Press the seam allowances toward the outer border. Join a red print O 5½" square to each end of the remaining outer-border strips. Press the seam allowances toward the squares. Join these strips to the top and bottom of the quilt top. The pieced quilt top should measure 62½" square, including the seam allowances.

Completing the Quilt

Layer and baste the quilt top, batting, and backing. Quilt the layers. The featured quilt was machine quilted with an assortment of simple designs to complement each individual block style set into the star centers. Concentric straight lines were stitched between the corner points of each large star block, and feathered wreaths were stitched onto the open areas defined by these diagonal lines. The small Mosaic Star and Cake Stand blocks were outlined, with closely spaced lines stitched onto the open background areas to fill the centers of each feathered wreath. A small pebbling design was stitched onto the inner background portion of the appliquéd border, the outer portion was stippled, and the appliqués and yo-yos were outlined to emphasize their shapes. A design of alternating loops was stitched onto the red sashing strips and the cream X portions of the outer border blocks, and double arced lines were quilted onto the large red squares and triangles in the outer border. Referring to "Kim's Chubby Binding" on page 127, or substituting your favorite method, use the red stripe binding strips to bind the quilt.

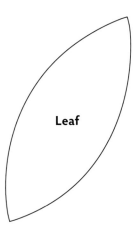

Leaf

Pattern does not include
seam allowance.

Once you've gathered a group of friends to exchange blocks, it's a good idea to establish some basic guidelines so everyone is on the same page and disappointments can be avoided. Agreeing on a few simple "rules" now will help ensure a successful swap. As a group . . .

- Determine which block you're going to exchange and the finished size of the block, if you choose to vary from the size given in the book.

- Decide on the color palette for the exchange, or opt to let each person select her or his own preferred color scheme.

- Determine the total number of blocks each person will receive. Once the number of blocks has been decided upon, divide it by the number of participants to calculate the number of blocks that should be in each swapped set. For instance, if the group feels that 30 blocks would make a nice-size quilt and you have five members in the group, divide 30 blocks by five participants for a total of six blocks. Each member will need to make five sets of six identical blocks—one set to keep and one set for each of the remaining group members. Keep in mind that if the quilt design or theme of the swap is scrappy, the blocks don't need to be identical, but they should follow the agreed-upon color guidelines regardless. (If the number of needed blocks doesn't divide equally, decide if everyone will make an extra block or if the recipient will make an extra block or two to complete her own set.)

- Decide whether fabrics should be prewashed or not. If prewashing is the chosen option, keep in mind that some participants may have allergies or be sensitive to fragrances; consider using fragrance-free soap or detergent and eliminating the use of fabric softener.

- Establish a realistic time frame for stitching the blocks, and establish a due date. Keep in mind that if the block design is intricate or the number of blocks to be stitched is large, it will take longer to complete the sets.

- Appoint a "hostess" for the exchange. Having a hostess will help the swap run smoothly because this person will make sure everyone receives a list of required materials and instructions for making the selected block. The hostess will establish a deadline for the exchange of the blocks, receive the stitched blocks for distribution to the members, and serve as the "go-to" person if anyone has questions along the way. In other words, the position of hostess is of mega-importance!

- Set any additional guidelines to help ensure your participants enjoy a successful swap.

This section provides how-to information for many of the techniques used to make the quilts and projects found in this book. For more details, please visit ShopMartingale.com/HowtoQuilt, where you can download free illustrated guidelines.

Cutting Bias Strips

Some projects in this book call for bias strips (lengths of cloth that have been cut diagonally rather than across the width of the fabric), which are usually used when a quilt features appliquéd stems and vines. The steps provided here describe Kim's preferred method for cutting these strips, as they enable her to work with a manageable size of fabric that produces strips approximately twice the cut length once they're unfolded. Another benefit of this method is that you can join the cut strips end to end to make one long strip, and then cut the exact pieces you need from this strip, resulting in little or no waste.

1. After pressing the fabric smooth, lay it in a single layer on a large cutting mat. Grasp one corner of the fabric and fold it back to form a layered triangle of any size you choose, aligning the top straight edge with the straight grain of the bottom layer of fabric.

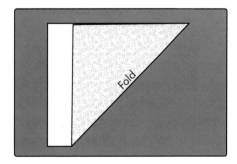

2. Rotate the folded fabric triangle to align the folded edge with a cutting line on your mat, ensuring the fold is resting evenly along the marked line to prevent a "dog-leg" curve in your strips after they've been cut and unfolded.

3. Use an acrylic ruler and rotary cutter to cut through the folded edge of the fabric a few inches in from one pointed end. With the ruler aligned with the lines of your cutting mat, begin cutting strips at measured intervals from this edge (using the dimensions given in the project instructions). If you reach the end of the folded edge of fabric and require additional strips, simply begin again at step 1 and repeat the process, using another corner of your cloth or squaring up the end from which you've been cutting.

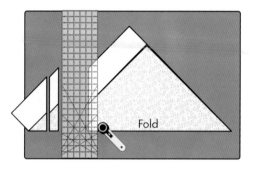

4. Square off the strip ends and trim them to the desired length, or sew multiple squared-off lengths together to achieve the length needed. Press the seam allowances to one side, all in the same direction. If you'll be using a bias bar to make bias-tube stems, joining the lengths with straight seams is best, because they allow the bias bar to slide easily through the sewn tubes in the direction the seams are resting without becoming caught on the seams.

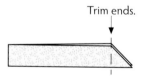

Trim ends.

Jo's Clipping Trick

This trick creates less bulk at the seam intersections of machine-stitched pieces, which will result in flatter blocks.

1. Clip up to the seamline through both layers of the seam allowance ¼" from each side of the seam intersection (the clips will be ½" apart).

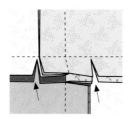

2. Press the clipped intersection open, and press the seam allowances in the direction they would like to lie.

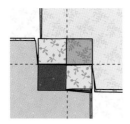

Jo's No-Waste Flying-Geese Method

Using this technique, you can quickly make four matching flying-geese units. You'll start with one large square, which will become the center triangle of the units, and four smaller squares, which will become the side triangles of the units.

1. Use a pencil and an acrylic ruler to draw a diagonal sewing line from corner to corner on the wrong side of the four small squares. Align two marked squares on opposite corners of the large square, right sides together. (The

squares will overlap in the center.) Sew a scant ¼" seam from both sides of the drawn line.

2. Cut the squares apart on the drawn line. Press the seam allowances toward the small triangles. You'll have two pieces that look like square hearts.

3. Place a marked small square on the corner of one large triangle as shown. Sew a scant ¼" from both sides of the drawn line.

4. Cut the pieces apart on the drawn line to make two flying-geese units. Press the seam allowances toward the small triangle. Repeat for the remaining unit to make a total of four flying-geese units.

Make 4.

Kim's Invisible Machine-Appliqué Technique

The results that can be achieved with invisible machine appliqué are fantastic because they closely resemble the look of needle turn, but the process is much quicker. In the information that follows, Kim will guide you through the techniques and share little pearls of wisdom she's learned from experience. In addition to your standard quiltmaking supplies, you'll need the following tools and products for this method:

- .004 monofilament thread in smoke and clear colors
- Awl or stiletto tool with a *sharp* point
- Bias bars in various widths
- Embroidery scissors with a fine, sharp point
- Freezer paper
- Iron with a sharp pressing point (travel-sized or mini appliqué irons work well for this technique)
- Liquid fabric glue, water-soluble and acid-free (Kim's favorite brand is Quilter's Choice Basting Glue by Beacon Adhesives)
- Open-toe presser foot
- Pressing board with a *firm* surface
- Sewing machine with adjustable tension control, capable of producing a tiny zigzag stitch
- Size 75/11 (or smaller) machine-quilting needles
- Tweezers with rounded tips

PREPARING PATTERN TEMPLATES

For projects with multiple appliqués made from one pattern, you can speed up the process by tracing around a sturdy template to make the pieces needed, rather than tracing over the pattern sheet numerous times. Keep in mind that complex shapes can be modified to fit your skill level— simply fatten up thin tips or redraw narrow inner curves to make them more appliqué friendly. Your end result will look essentially the same, but the shapes will be much easier to work with.

Any time a template is used, only one is needed, as it's simply a tracing tool to easily duplicate the pattern shape for the remaining appliqué steps. Kim makes templates from freezer paper (which eliminates the need to buy template plastic) using these easy steps:

1. Cut a single piece of freezer paper about twice as large as your shape. Use a pencil to trace the pattern onto one end of the nonwaxy side of the paper. Fold the freezer paper in half, waxy sides together, and use a hot, dry iron (Kim places hers on the "cotton" setting) to fuse the folded paper layers together.

2. Cut out the shape on the drawn line, taking care to duplicate it accurately.

PREPARING PAPER PATTERN PIECES

Pattern *pieces* are used differently than pattern *templates:* pattern pieces are individual paper shapes that you'll use to prepare the appliqués from fabric. Always cut your paper pattern pieces on the drawn lines; you'll add seam allowances later when the shapes are cut from fabric. As you cut the paper pattern pieces, move the paper, rather than the scissors, to cut smooth edges.

Use the prepared template (or pattern sheet, if you're preparing fewer than a dozen pieces) to trace the number of pattern pieces needed onto the nonwaxy side of a piece of freezer paper. To easily make multiple pattern pieces, stack the freezer paper (up to eight layers deep for simple shapes, and four to six layers deep for more complex shapes) with the waxy sides facing down; pin through the centers of the shapes to anchor them and prevent shifting, or use staples at regular intervals slightly outside the shape in the background. Cut out the pattern pieces on the drawn lines and discard the background areas.

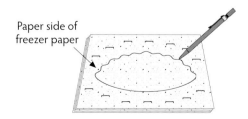

Paper side of freezer paper

To prepare mirror-image pieces, trace the pattern onto the nonwaxy side of one end of a strip of freezer paper, and then fold it accordion style in widths to fit your shape. Anchor the layers together as previously described and cut out the shape. When you separate the pieces, every other shape will be a mirror image.

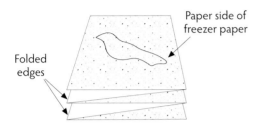

Folded edges

Paper side of freezer paper

Multiple pattern pieces for shapes that have an obvious direction (such as a bird) should be prepared by stacking individual freezer paper pieces waxy side down and cutting as described previously.

PREPARING APPLIQUÉS

1. Apply a small amount of fabric glue stick to the center of the dull paper side of each pattern piece before affixing it to the wrong side of the fabric. Place patterns shiny side *up*, leaving approximately ½" between each shape for seam allowances. Position the longest lines or curves of each shape on the diagonal, because the resulting bias edges are easier to work with than straight-grain edges when pressing the seam allowances over the paper pattern pieces.

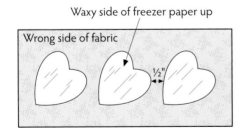

Waxy side of freezer paper up

Wrong side of fabric

½"

2. Using embroidery scissors, cut out each shape, adding an approximate ¼" seam allowance around the paper. For this technique, more is actually better when it comes to seam allowances, as cutting too scant a seam allowance will make the fabric more difficult to work with. Any seam-allowance section that

feels too bulky can be trimmed a bit as you being pressing, but you can't make scant seam allowances bigger.

When turning seam allowances to the back of an appliqué to press and finish the edges, Kim recommends leaving the seam allowances of outer curves and points unclipped. The seam allowances of inner points or pronounced inner curves should be clipped once at the center position, stopping two or three threads away from the paper edge. If you're unsure whether an inner curve is pronounced enough to need a clip, try pressing it without one—if the fabric easily follows the shape of the curve and lies flat, you've eliminated a step!

Clip inner points to paper edge.

PRESSING APPLIQUÉS

The steps that follow will help you produce finished appliqués with smoothly turned-under edges that closely resemble needle turn. Keep in mind that for each shape, you'll want to work along the appliqué edge on the side that's farthest away from you, rotating the appliqué toward the point of your iron as you work in one direction from start to finish.

The smaller the shape or curvier the edges are, the smaller the increments should be as you rotate and press your way around the piece—this will enable the fabric to smoothly hug the shape of your appliqué for smooth, flawless results. Always begin pressing along a straight edge or a gentle curve, never at a point or a corner, and rotate the appliqué toward the iron as previously suggested, because this will direct the seam allowance of any points toward your "smart" hand (which you'll later use to hold the awl or stiletto to fine-tune and finish any points).

1. Begin at a straight or gently curved edge and work your way around the entire shape in

one direction. Use the pad of your finger to smooth the fabric seam allowance over onto the waxy side of the paper pattern piece, following with the point of a hot, dry iron (Kim uses the cotton setting) and *firmly* press it in place. The weight of the iron will work together with the heat to anchor the seam to the pattern piece. To avoid puckered appliqué edges, always draw the seam allowance slightly backward toward the last section pressed. Kim likes to rest the point of her iron on each newly pressed section of seam allowance, holding it in place as she draws the next section over onto the paper pattern piece. Allowing the iron to rest in place while you work will lengthen the amount of time the fabric receives heat, helping the cloth to fuse more firmly to the paper.

Direct seam allowance
toward center of shape.

2. For sharp outer points, press the seam allowance so the folded edge of the fabric extends beyond the first side of the pattern point, snugging the fabric firmly up against the paper edge. Fold over the seam allowance of the remaining side of the point and continue pressing. After the seam allowance of the entire piece has been pressed, apply a small amount of fabric glue stick to the bottom of the folded flap of fabric seam allowance at the point. If the seam-allowance flap will be visible from the front of the appliqué, use the point of an awl or stiletto to drag the fabric in and away from the appliqué edge (not down from the point, as this will blunt it), and touch it with the point of a hot iron to heat set the glue and fuse it in place.

For narrow points, roll the seam allowances under slightly as you draw them in from the edge with the awl; this will enable the seam allowance to be completely hidden from the front of the appliqué.

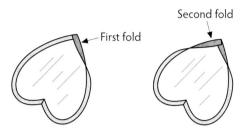

Second fold
First fold

One more tip for achieving beautiful, sharp appliqué points is to take care that your pressed seam allowance hugs the paper edge on both sides of any given point. Kim has often found that when a point is less than perfect, it's because the fabric seam allowance has flared away from the paper pattern piece, resulting in a "mushy" point. Ensuring the cloth always hugs the pattern piece will help produce crisp, precise points.

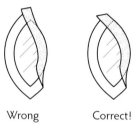

Wrong   Correct!

3. To prepare an inner point or pronounced inner curve, stop pressing the seam allowance just shy of the center clipped section. Reaching under the appliqué at the clip, use the pad of your finger or the point of an awl to draw the clipped section of fabric snugly onto the paper, following immediately with the iron to fuse the cloth in place onto the paper.

Always turn your prepared appliqué over to the front to evaluate your pressing and adjust any areas that could be improved. Tiny imperfections can be smoothed by nudging them with the point of your hot iron, and more pronounced imperfections can be loosened and re-pressed from the back.

MAKING BIAS-TUBE STEMS AND VINES

To achieve finished stems and vines that can be curved flawlessly and don't require the seam allowances to be turned under, Kim uses bias tubes. After cutting the strips specified in the project instructions (and referring to "Cutting Bias Strips" on page 114 for guidelines), prepare them as follows:

1. With *wrong* sides together, fold the strip in half lengthwise and stitch a scant ¼" (a few threads less than a true ¼") from the long raw edges to form a tube. Using a scant ¼" seam allowance often eliminates the need to trim the seam allowance and allows the bias bar to slide through the sewn fabric tube more easily.) For any stem sewn from a strip 1" wide or less, you'll likely need to trim the seam allowance to approximately ⅛" so that it will be hidden when the stem is viewed from the front.

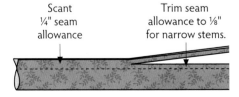

Scant ¼" seam allowance

Trim seam allowance to ⅛" for narrow stems.

2. Because of seam allowance differences and varying fabric weights, the best bias-bar width for each project can vary from person to person, even for stems of the same size. Ultimately, Kim has found it's best to simply choose a bar that will fit comfortably into the sewn tube, and then slide it along as you press the stem, positioning the seam allowance so it's resting flat to one side, not open, and resting in such a way that it won't be visible from the front.

Bias bar

3. Remove the bias bar and place small dots of liquid basting glue at approximately ½" to 1" intervals along the seamline underneath the layers of the pressed seam allowance; use a hot, dry iron on the wrong side of the stem, allowing it to rest on each area of the stem for two or three seconds, to heat set the glue and fuse the seam allowance in place.

BASTING APPLIQUÉS

Invisible machine appliqué, like traditional hand appliqué, is sewn in layers from the bottom to the top. Keep in mind as you lay out and baste your appliqués that it's a good practice to leave approximately ½" between the outermost appliqués of your design and the raw edge of your background, because this will preserve an intact margin of space around each piece after the quilt top has been assembled.

1. Lay out the prepared appliqués on the background to ensure that everything fits and is to your liking. As you lay out your pieces, any appliqué with a raw edge that will be overlapped by another piece (such as a stem) should be overlapped by approximately ¼" to prevent fraying.

2. Remove all but the bottom appliqués and pin or baste them in place. Kim prefers to baste with liquid glue for fabric because there are no pins to stitch around or remove and the appliqués won't shift or cause the background cloth to shrink as it's stitched. Follow these steps for glue basting your appliqués:

   Without shifting the appliqué from its position, fold over one half of the shape to expose the back and place small dots of liquid basting glue along the fabric seam allowance (not the freezer-paper pattern piece) at approximately ½" to 1" intervals. Firmly push the glue-basted portion of the appliqué in place with your hand and repeat with the remaining half of the shape. From the back, use a hot, dry iron to heat set the glue.

PREPARING YOUR SEWING MACHINE

Monofilament thread produces results that are nearly invisible and it's easy to use once you know how to prepare your sewing machine. Always be sure to match your monofilament thread to your appliqué, not your background, choosing the smoke color for medium and dark prints and clear for bright colors and pastels. If you're not sure which color is the best choice, lay a strand of each thread over your print to audition the results. Whenever possible, use the upright spool pin position on your sewing machine for the monofilament, as this will facilitate a smooth, even feed.

1. Use a size 75/11 (or smaller) machine-quilting needle in your sewing machine and thread it with monofilament. Prints with a subtle texture, and often batiks, can make needle holes more visible, so if this occurs, try substituting a smaller needle, such as a 60/8.

2. Wind the bobbin with all-purpose, neutral-colored thread. A 50-weight (or heavier) thread works well for this technique in most sewing machines, as it will resist sliding through the cloth and pulling up through the surface of your appliqués. Also, keep in mind that prewound bobbins, while convenient, can sometimes make it difficult to achieve perfectly balanced tension for this technique.

   Note: *If your machine's bobbin case features a special eye for use with embroidery techniques, threading your bobbin thread through this opening will often provide additional tension control to perfectly regulate your stitches.*

3. Program your sewing machine to the zigzag stitch, adjust the width and length to achieve a tiny stitch as shown below (keeping in mind that your inner stitches should land two or three threads inside your appliqué, with your outer stitches piercing the background immediately next to the appliqué), and reduce the tension setting. For many sewing machines, a width, length, and tension setting of 1 produces the perfect stitch.

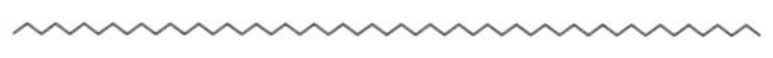

Approximate stitch size

STITCHING THE APPLIQUÉS

Before stitching your first invisible machine-appliqué project, it's a good idea to experiment with a simple pattern shape to find the best settings for your sewing machine. Keep your test piece as a quick reference for future projects, making a note directly on the background fabric as to your machine's width, length, and tension settings. Also, if you routinely use more than one type of thread in your bobbin, you should make a note of the thread that was used for your test piece—if the thread in your bobbin is changed for a different type, the balance of your components may change as well, and your settings may need to be adjusted.

1. Slide the basted appliqué under the presser foot from front to back to direct the threads behind the machine, positioning it to the left of the needle.

2. Begin at a straight or gently curved edge. Place your fingertip over the monofilament tail as your machine takes two or three stitches. Release the threads and continue zigzag stitching around the shape, with inner stitches landing on the appliqué and outer stitches piercing the background immediately next to the appliqué. Train your eyes to watch the outer stitches while you sew to keep your appliqué positioned correctly, and the inner stitches will naturally fall into place. After a short distance, pause and carefully clip the monofilament tail close to the background.

Stitch your appliqué at a slow to moderate speed to maintain good control, stopping and pivoting as often as needed to keep the edge of your shape feeding straight toward the needle. Whenever possible, pivot with the needle down inside the appliqué, because the paper pattern piece will stabilize the shape and prevent it from stretching or becoming distorted.

- If dots of bobbin thread appear along the top surface edge of your appliqué as you stitch, further adjust the tension settings on your machine (usually lower) until they disappear.

- The stitches should look like a true zigzag pattern on the wrong side of your work. If the monofilament thread is visible underneath your appliqué from the back, or the stitches appear loose or loopy, adjust the tension settings (usually higher) until they're secure.

3. To firmly secure an inner appliqué point, stitch to the position where the inner stitch rests exactly on the inner point of the appliqué and stop. Pivot the fabric, and with the appliqué inner point at a right angle to the needle, continue stitching. For pieces with

inner points that seem delicate, Kim often gives a little resistance to her piece as it's feeding under the needle to enable a couple of stitches to drop into the appliqué and secure it well.

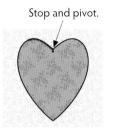 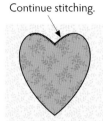

Stop and pivot.   Continue stitching.

4. To secure an outer point, stitch to the position where the outer stitch lands exactly next to the appliqué point in the background and stop. Pivot the fabric and continue stitching along the next side of the shape. As you begin sewing again, a second stitch will drop into the point of the appliqué.

Stop and pivot.   Continue stitching.

5. Continue stitching around the edge of the appliqué until you overlap your starting point by approximately ¼". End with a locking stitch if your machine offers this feature, placing it where it will best be hidden. For machines without a locking stitch, extend your overlapped area to about ½" and your appliqué will remain well secured.

6. From time to time, evaluate the stitch placement along your appliqué edges to ensure you're achieving the best possible results. To do this, hold a completed appliqué piece up to the light and view it with the light shining from behind. A properly stitched appliqué will have a ring of tiny needle holes encircling the appliqué in the background cloth. If your results appear different, then adjustments to the placement of your work under the needle should be made as you stitch future pieces.

STRING APPLIQUÉ

When two or more appliqués are in close proximity on the same layer, Kim suggests stitching the first appliqué as instructed in "Stitching the Appliqués" (page 120), but instead of clipping the threads when you finish, lift the presser foot and slide the background to the next appliqué without lifting it from the sewing machine surface. Lower the presser foot and resume stitching the next appliqué, remembering to end with a locking stitch or overlap your starting position by ¼" to ½". After the cluster of appliqués has been stitched, carefully clip the threads between each.

REMOVING PAPER PATTERN PIECES

On the wrong side of the stitched appliqué, use embroidery scissors to carefully pinch and cut through the fabric approximately ¼" inside the appliqué seam. Trim away the background fabric, leaving a generous ¼" seam allowance. Grasp the appliqué edge between the thumb and forefinger of one hand, and grab the seam allowances immediately opposite with the other hand. Give a gentle but firm tug to free the paper edge. Next, use your fingertip to loosen the glue anchoring the pattern piece to the fabric; peel away and discard the paper. Any paper that remains in the appliqué corners can be pulled out with a pair of tweezers. Please rest easy knowing that cutting away the fabric behind an appliqué won't weaken the quilt top in any way—this appliqué method is very secure, and it produces finished quilts that are soft and pliable, even with multiple layers of fabric.

COMPLETING THE MACHINE APPLIQUÉ PROCESS

Working from the bottom layer to the top, continue basting and stitching the appliqués until each one has been secured in place, remembering to remove the paper pattern pieces before adding each new layer. Keep in mind that it isn't necessary to stitch any edge that will be overlapped by another piece. If needed, *briefly* press your finished work from the back to ensure the seam allowances lie smooth and flat. Always take care not to apply direct heat to the front of your appliqués, as this could weaken the monofilament threads.

Kim's Wool-Appliqué Technique

Wool is a really fun, fast, and forgiving fabric to work with, and Kim especially loves the magic that happens when it's used in combination with traditional cotton fabrics. Wool that's been felted has a soft, densely woven feel to the cloth and it resists raveling as you work with it. Kim suggests that you use only 100% wool and, as a general rule, avoid worsted wool because it doesn't felt well and can be challenging to work with. You can usually identify worsted wool by its hard, flat weave, and you'll often find it used for garments such as men's suits.

For Kim's method of appliquéing with wool, you'll need the following items in addition to your standard quiltmaking supplies:

- #8 or #12 perle cotton in colors to match or complement your wool
- Embroidery needle (Kim uses a size 5 needle)
- Freezer paper
- Liquid fabric glue, water-soluble and acid-free (Kim's favorite brand is Quilter's Choice Basting Glue by Beacon Adhesives)
- Paper-backed fusible web (Kim likes the results achieved when using HeatnBond Lite)
- Sharp scissors with a fine point
- Thimble

FELTING WOOL

If your wool hasn't been felted, this is easy to do. Wash similar-hued wool pieces in the washing machine on the longest cycle using a hot-water wash and a cold-water rinse. (Skim the surface of the water once or twice during the cycle to prevent loose fibers from clogging the drain.)

Next, dry the wool in your dryer, again using the longest and hottest setting. Remove the dry wool promptly to help prevent wrinkles from forming.

As an added safety measure, wash and dry vividly colored pieces separately if you suspect they might lose dye, and never wash wool that's been overdyed, because it will almost certainly bleed color. It's better to be safe and ask rather than to guess and be sorry. Finally, never wash wool that's been included as part of a kitted project, because it can continue to shrink and you may find yourself without enough wool to complete your project.

PREPARING WOOL APPLIQUÉS

When working with wool, Kim likes to use a fusible-appliqué technique for the preparation steps, liquid fabric glue for basting the layers of wool together, and perle cotton and an embroidery needle as she stitches the pieces. The combination of fusible web and the liquid glue produces ideal results because the iron-on adhesive finishes and stabilizes the underside of the wool edges to reduce fraying, while the glue-basted edges hold the layers of wool together beautifully for easy stitching without pinning.

Keep in mind, when you're working with wool appliqués using the technique that follows, that your finished shapes will appear backward and be reversed on your quilt if they're directional and aren't perfectly symmetrical.

1. Trace each appliqué shape the number of times indicated in the project instructions onto the paper side of your iron-on adhesive,

leaving approximately ½" between each shape. For projects with numerous identical shapes (or nonsymmetrical shapes that need to be reversed), make a template as instructed in "Preparing Pattern Templates" (page 116) and use it to trace the required number of pieces. Remember that for this method you'll need one traced iron-on adhesive shape for each appliqué.

2. Cut out each shape approximately ¼" *outside* the drawn lines, and then cut away the center portion of the shape approximately ¼" *inside* the drawn lines to eliminate bulk and keep the shape pliable after the appliqué has been stitched. For added stability in large shapes, leave a narrow strip of paper across the middle of the shape as you cut away the excess center portion, because this will act as a bridge to connect the sides and prevent distortion as you lay out your shape onto the wool.

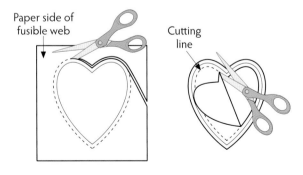

Paper side of fusible web

Cutting line

3. Following the manufacturer's instructions, fuse each shape, paper side *up*, to the *wrong* side of the fabric. After the fabric has cooled,

123

cut out each shape exactly on the drawn lines. To protect the fusible adhesive and prevent the fabric appliqué edges from fraying, Kim leaves the paper backing on prepared pieces until she's ready to use them. To easily remove the paper backing, loosen an inside edge of the paper with a needle and peel it away.

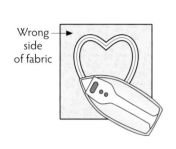 

Wrong side of fabric

STITCHING WOOL APPLIQUÉS

Kim prefers the overhand stitch when appliquéing wool shapes because it's quick to stitch, uses less thread, and the stitches stay in place without rolling over the appliqué edge.

Work from the top layer to the bottom to stitch any wool pieces with multiple layers (such as a stack of pennies) into units *before* adding them to the project background, to simplify the sewing and eliminate the need to stitch through multiple layers of wool. Once the layered units have been prepared, the remaining portions of the appliqué designs can be stitched to the background, working from the bottom layer to the top.

1. Lay out your appliqués, including any stitched appliqué units, on your background to ensure everything fits and is to your liking. Set aside all but the bottom pieces, remove the paper backing on each remaining piece, and glue baste them in place, referring to "Basting Appliqués" (page 119) and applying small dots of liquid glue directly onto the narrow margin of fusible adhesive that rims each shape.

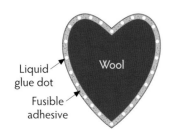

Liquid glue dot

Wool

Fusible adhesive

2. Use an embroidery needle threaded with a single knotted strand of #8 or #12 perle cotton to overhand stitch the pieces in place.

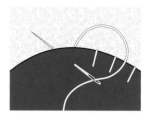

Overhand stitch

3. Remove the paper backings from the appliqués needed for the next layer of the design, and then position, baste, and stitch them in place, ensuring that any appliqué overlapping another piece does so by at least ¼". Continue working from the bottom layer to the top in this manner to complete the appliqué design. It isn't necessary to cut away the backs of any appliqués stitched from wool.

Jo's Back-Basting Needle-Turn Appliqué

For this hand appliqué method, you'll be creating the appliqués directly from the design that you've traced onto the background fabric. With this technique the pieces will be correctly positioned and the appliqués will lie flatter.

You'll need the following tools and products for this method:

- Fine-line permanent marker (Jo likes Pigma Micron sizes 03 and 05)
- Mechanical pencil with 0.7 mm or 0.9 mm lead (a finer lead, like 0.5 mm, will drop into the weave and is more apt to stretch the fabric)
- Clover fine-line white marking pen
- YLI or Gütterman waxed quilting thread in a color that contrasts with appliqué fabrics (yellow is Jo's favorite)
- A good pair of small, sharp scissors for cutting fabric and clipping threads (Jo prefers Dovo 5" sewing scissors)
- 50- or 60-weight, 3-ply thread in colors to match the appliqués

- Jeana Kimball's size 9 and 11 Straw needles (jeanakimballquilter.com)
- Needle threader (Jo highly recommends the Clover double needle threader)
- Light box (not mandatory, but helpful)

1. Cut out the background piece at least 1" larger than the finished size. For Parkersburg (page 56), the additional 1" is already included in the cutting dimensions.

2. Place the pattern on a light box or other light source so the reversed side is face up. Center the background piece, wrong side up, over the traced image. If you can't see the pattern through the fabric, remove the fabric and use a black Pigma pen to trace the image through to the wrong side of the paper pattern.

3. With the mechanical pencil, trace the design onto the wrong side of the background fabric.

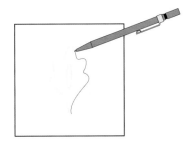

Position pattern on the front
and trace onto the back.

4. Figure out the appliqué stitching sequence. Just like with any other method, stitch the shapes that go under other pieces first.

5. Cut a piece from the appropriate fabric that's large enough to cover the entire piece to be appliquéd, with enough extra for seam allowance. Place the piece on the right side of the background fabric over the shape to be appliquéd. Hold the background fabric up to the light so you can make sure the correct area is covered. Pin the fabric in place.

6. Thread a size 9 Straw needle with a length of wax thread, but don't knot it. Using a short running stitch (9 to 10 stitches per inch) and working from the wrong side, baste the

appliqué fabric to the background, stitching directly on the marked line of the shape. Start on a straight edge if possible, and leave a 2" thread tail at the beginning and end or anytime you start and end with a new thread.

Position motif fabric on the front and pin from the back.
Baste with small running stitches exactly on drawn line.

7. Turn over the unit to the right side. Using small, sharp scissors, cut away the excess appliqué fabric, leaving a fat ⅛" seam allowance. Jo recommends letting the piece rest for 24 hours to give the perforations created by the basting time to set. You won't see the perforation when you stitch, but the appliqué will turn under nicely along the stitching line.

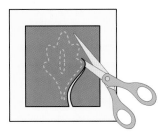

8. Thread a size 11 Straw needle with an 18" length of 50- or 60-weight thread to match the appliqué fabric. Knot one end of the thread. You'll be working with a single strand. Starting at a basting thread tail and preferably on a straight edge, use your threaded sewing needle to pull the basting thread to the top, and then pull out two or three stitches.

9. Insert the needle into the perforation line from the wrong side of the appliqué fabric. This will hide the knot between the appliqué and the background fabric. Use your needle to turn under the seam allowance. See how the fabric turns under along the "basting" line?

10. Insert the needle into the background fabric as close as possible to where the thread came out of the fold. Take about a 1/16" stitch, coming up through the folded edge of the appliqué. Just barely catch the folded edge of the appliqué piece so that the thread won't be seen.

11. Take a few more stitches in the same manner and then remove a few more basting stitches. Continue stitching around the entire shape in this way, removing only a couple of basting stitches at a time so your appliqué edges will be smooth. To end your stitching, insert the needle next to the appliqué edge and pull the thread to the back. Wrap the thread around the needle twice, hold the needle down next to the fabric, and then pull the needle and thread through to create a knot just on top of the fabric. Insert your needle where the thread came out, and pull to bury the knot between the background fabric and the appliqué fabric. Carefully clip the thread next to the fabric.

12. Continue adding appliqués, working from the bottom layer to the top. Jo doesn't cut away any of the background fabric behind the appliqués; she likes adhering to the way many antique quilts were done. Ultimately, however, it's a matter of personal choice.

Hand Quilting

To hand quilt your project, place the layered quilt top in a hoop or frame and follow these steps:

1. Thread your needle with an approximately 18" length of quilting thread and knot one end. Insert the needle into the quilt top about 1" from where you wish to begin quilting, sliding it through the layers and bringing it up through the top; gently tug until the knot is drawn down into the layer of batting.

2. Take small, even stitches through the layers until you near the end of the thread. Make a knot in the thread about 1/8" from the quilt top. Insert and slide the needle through the batting layer, bringing it back up about 1" beyond your last stitch, tugging gently until the knot disappears; carefully clip the thread.

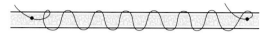
Hand-quilting stitch

Binding

For information on traditional double-fold binding, go to ShopMartingale.com/HowtoQuilt. See below for Jo's and Kim's preferred binding methods.

JO'S SINGLE-FOLD BINDING

Because Jo's quilts are generally small, she likes to use a single-fold binding, feeling that a double-fold binding is too heavy for most small quilts. To prevent the binding from stretching, she recommends using a walking foot or built-in dual-feed mechanism when attaching binding.

1. Cut 1⅛"-wide strips across the width of the fabric (selvage to selvage). Using a diagonal seam, join the short ends, right sides together, to make one long strip. Press the seam allowances open.

2. With right sides together, align the long raw edge of the binding with the raw edge of the quilt top. Beginning about 4" to 5" from the binding end, sew the binding to the quilt top. Stop sewing about 5" or 6" from the beginning of the strip and remove the quilt from the machine.

3. Fold the beginning of the binding strip toward the center of the quilt at a 45° angle.

Next, fold the end of the binding strip toward the edge of the quilt at a 45° angle, leaving a gap of about ⅛" between the folds; press. This gap will help the binding lie nice and flat.

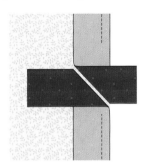

4. Align the fold lines, right sides together, and pin them in place. Sew on the fold line, backstitching at the beginning and end.

5. Trim the excess binding strip, leaving a ¼" seam allowance. Press the seam allowances open. Finish sewing the binding in place.

6. Trim the batting and backing even with the quilt edges. Fold the binding away from the quilt and press the raw edge under ¼". Fold the binding over the quilt edge and pin it in place so it covers the first stitching, mitering the corners as you go when turning.

7. Blindstitch the binding by hand to the quilt back, using small, closely spaced stitches, and being careful not to stitch through to the front of the quilt. Take three or four stitches on the folds of the mitered corners to secure them.

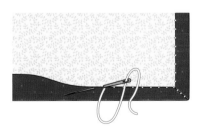

KIM'S CHUBBY BINDING

Kim loves the look of "chubby" binding because it uses strips with a single fold for less bulk and produces a wide strip of color to beautifully frame the back of the quilt. For this method, you'll need a bias-tape maker for 1"-wide, double-fold tape. Kim usually uses binding strips that have been

cut on the straight of grain, rather than the bias, because she feels this gives her quilt edges added stability. For scrappy bindings, she loves the look achieved when the strips are sewn together end to end using straight rather than diagonal seams.

1. Cut the strips 2" wide and join them end to end. Next, slide the pieced strip through the bias-tape maker, pressing the folds with a hot, dry iron as they emerge so that the raw edges meet in the center. As the tape maker slides along the pieced strip, the seam allowances will automatically be directed to one side as they're pressed, resulting in one less step!

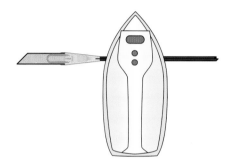

2. Open the fold of the strip along the top edge only. Turn the beginning raw end under ½" and finger-press the fold. Starting along one side of the quilt top, not at a corner, align the unfolded raw edge of the binding with the raw edge of the quilt, and stitch the binding in place.

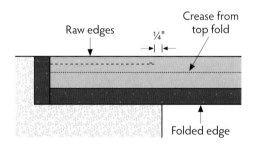

Raw edges   ¼"   Crease from top fold

Folded edge

3. When you approach your starting point, cut the end to extend 1" beyond the folded edge and complete the stitching.

4. Bring the wide folded edge of the binding to the back and hand stitch it (including the mitered folds at the corners) using a whipstitch. The raw end of the strip will now be encased within the binding.

Kim Diehl

After falling in love with a sampler quilt pattern in the late 1990s, Kim impulsively purchased it, taught herself the steps needed to make the project, and realized she was smitten with quiltmaking. Kim's favorite quilt designs combine traditionally inspired patchwork and appliqué, and she loves stitching her projects from richly hued prints using modern timesaving techniques.

In addition to authoring her Simple series of books with Martingale, Kim designs quilting fabric collections and Simple Whatnots Club projects in her signature scrappy style for Henry Glass & Co.

Since retiring from an extensive travel and teaching schedule in 2015, Kim enjoys spending her days at home once again and doing what she loves most—designing quilts and fabrics, baking and stitching, and being a nana to her grandbabies.

Jo Morton

Jo Morton is a quiltmaker, fabric designer, teacher, author, and lecturer. Her use of color and design, as well as her fine stitchery, give her quilts the feeling of being made in the nineteenth century. She determined early on that if she ever hoped to make all the quilts she wanted to, they would have to be small, and small works perfectly in the 1929 tiny bungalow where she lives.

Jo is well-known for her "Jo's Little Women Club" patterns, available through participating quilt shops since 2003. Her quilts have appeared in numerous magazines, and she's made television appearances on HGTV's *Simply Quilts*, PBS's *Love of Quilting*, and *The Quilt Show*, which airs on the Internet via subscription.

Jo lives in Nebraska City with her husband, Russ, and her kitty, Chloe. Visit her at JoMortonQuilts.com to learn more. Follow Jo on Instagram at joquilts.